Essential
Czech Republic
(with excursions into Slovakia)

by
MICHAEL IVORY

Michael Ivory's interest in Central and Eastern Europe
goes back to study and travel in the late 1950s. After
taking modern languages at Oxford, he qualified as a
landscape architect and town planner, and now works
as a freelance lecturer and travel writer.

AA

Produced by AA Publishing

**Written by Michael Ivory
Peace and Quiet section
by Paul Sterry
Original photography
by Jon Wyand**

Edited, designed and produced by AA Publishing. Maps © The Automobile Association 1994

Distributed in the United Kingdom by AA Publishing, Fanum House, Basingstoke, Hampshire, RG21 2EA.

The contents of this publication are believed correct at the time of printing. Nevertheless, the publishers cannot be held responsible for any errors or omissions, or for changes in details given in this guide or for the consequences of any reliance on the information provided by the same. Assessments of attractions, hotels, restaurants and so forth are based upon the author's own experience and, therefore, descriptions given in this guide necessarily contain an element of subjective opinion which may not reflect the publisher's opinion or dictate a reader's own experience on another occasion.
We have tried to ensure accuracy in this guide, but things do change and we would be grateful if readers would advise us of any inaccuracies they may encounter.

A CIP catalogue record for this book is available from the British Library.

ISBN 0 7495 0711 X

Published by AA Publishing, which is a trading name of Automobile Association Developments Limited, whose registered office is Fanum House, Basingstoke, Hampshire, RG21 2EA.
Registered number 1878835.

Colour separation: L C Repro, Aldermaston

Printed by: Printers Trento, S.R.L., Italy

Front cover picture: Cheb, Western Bohemia

Country Distinguishing Signs

On some maps, international distinguishing signs have been used to indicate the location of countries which surround Portugal . Thus:

Ⓐ = Austria
Ⓓ = Federal Republic of Germany
Ⓗ = Hungary
Ⓟ = Poland
Ⓡ= Romania

Contents

This book employs a simple rating system to help choose which places to visit:

✓	'top ten'
♦♦♦	do not miss
♦♦	see if you can
♦	worth seeing if you have time

Introduction and Background

INTRODUCTION

Even before the fall of Communism in 1989, 'Golden Prague' had been attracting an ever-growing host of visitors from abroad, curious to find out for themselves if it really was what its admirers proclaimed – the most beautiful city north of the Alps. Now that the barriers are down, Prague has become one of Europe's favourite tourist destinations. Every age from early medieval to modern has helped shape an architectural heritage which, spared by war and by redevelopment, has remained miraculously intact. To stroll through this unique city is to experience a harmony which has vanished from most other places of its size. But Prague is not simply a glorious monument to its own eventful history; it was also the seat of the Velvet Revolution, which overthrew a rigid regime without violence, the focal point of a gifted people who are quickly taking their

Tyn Church towers over Prague's glorious Old Town

TŘEBOŇ · LÁZNĚ (ČŠ
STRÁŽ N. NEŽ.
JINDŘICHŮV HRADE
1988

SVĚT (RYB.)
SPOLSKÝ RYB. (Ž
BOROVANY
1988

TŘEBOŇ · LÁZNĚ (ČŠ
HODĚJOV (RYB.)·ŽLL
JEMČINA
1988

ŠUSTŮV POMNÍ
NA TŘEBOŇSKÉ CE
NOVÉ HRADY (ČS
1988

ŠUSTŮV POMNÍ
RUDA (ROZC.)
JÍLOVICE (ČSD)
1988

TŘEBOŇ · LÁZNĚ (Č
DLOUHÝ MOST
STAŇKOV (ČSAD)
1988

*Pointing the way –
Czech roadsigns*

place in a Europe from which they were excluded for more than 40 years. No language barrier will stop you sensing the dynamic currents of cultural, political and economic vitality which are refreshing the life of this capital city of a new republic.

The Czech Republic is not just Prague. Beyond the capital is a whole country waiting to be discovered, endowed with a wealth of attractions which would be the envy of many better-known places. Most people have heard of the famous Bohemian spas, still best known under their German names of Carlsbad (Karlovy Vary) or Marienbad (Mariánské Lázně), but few are familiar with the exquisite little episcopal city of Kroměříž, or with the tranquil pool-studded landscape of southern Bohemia. In the Middle Ages the Czech lands were one of the richest parts of Europe; monarchs founded an array of planned towns, while aristocrats built their castles on sites seemingly chosen as much for their beauty as for their impregnability. The passage of time has lent many of these ancient settlements and strongholds further layers of fascination; around the medieval town square, with its plague column or fountain, will stand burghers' houses of all styles and periods – Renaissance, baroque, Empire, even Art Nouveau – while many a medieval fortress will have acquired luxurious extensions from its owners' periods of prosperity. Added to this exceptional heritage is a church architecture as glorious as any in Europe.

The environment of the Czech Republic has had a bad press of late, with the devastation caused by reckless industrialisation recorded in several articles and television features. While some of the country's splendid forested uplands have suffered grievously from air pollution, most of the countryside is still unspoiled, its rivers, rock formations, woods and fields providing a charming counterpoint to the pleasures of towns, villages and country houses.

Bear in mind when planning your visit that the country is recovering from 40 years of what has been described as 'abnormal development'. Between 1948, the date of the Communist *coup*

Prague, 1870

d'état, and 1989, the year of the Velvet
Revolution, the nation's life was forced into
tightly constricted patterns, from which it tried
and failed to free itself during the short-lived
Prague Spring of 1968. The economy was
planned, individual initiative suppressed, and
much talent lost. This has left a heritage of
crumbling infrastructure and a rudimentary
service sector. Alongside lovingly conserved
or immaculately restored buildings, don't be
surprised to find edifices apparently on the
verge of collapse. The tickling in your nostrils
is probably caused by smoke from the soft
brown coal dug from open pits in north
Bohemia and used everywhere as a not very
efficient fuel. Under the old regime, hotels,
restaurants and shops tended to be run for the
convenience of the personnel and
management, with little attention paid to the
customer. To the uninitiated, this could be
interpreted as rudeness, though indifference
would probably be a fairer description. A lot
has changed, with privatisation of state
enterprises of all kinds and the establishment of
many new ones. Nevertheless, especially
outside Prague, you will come across vestiges
of the old system. There will not always be a
café where you would expect one, and the
hotel may not have all the facilities you might
expect. This is more than compensated for, not
only by the beauty of the surroundings but also
by the Czechs themselves, a wry race whose
company you are bound to enjoy as you
explore their small but fascinating country.

Woodlands in Bohemia

BACKGROUND

The Land

The Czech lands, particularly Bohemia, are blessed with very clearly defined natural frontiers in the form of well-forested mountain ranges whose ridges divide the country from its other Central European neighbours, Polish Silesia to the north, German Saxony and Bavaria to the northwest and southwest and Slovakia to the east. Only in the south do the lowlands, shared by Moravia with Austria, fail to give the border this precise geographical definition. These boundaries have rarely acted as barriers; ancient routeways were traced across the mountains, while the country's great rivers have encouraged trade and movement up and downstream. All of Bohemia drains into the Vltava and Labe (Elbe), flowing to the North Sea via Dresden and Hamburg; all of Moravia drains into the River Morava, which joins the mighty Danube between Vienna and Bratislava. Within the highland rim spread the 'woods and fields' celebrated by Smetana. Apart from the interminable tracts of sugarbeet in the valley of the Labe, woodlands are everywhere, mainly of spruce and pine but also of beech and birch, especially along the dramatic river gorges. Looking out from the woodland edge over the sweeping expanses of pasture and arable land that collectivisation has created are little cabins perched on tall timber legs that serve as huntsmen's hides; the country is rich in game, creatures such as boar having increased in numbers during recent years. The sometimes dull landscape of modern agriculture, with its open fields and huge farm buildings, is relieved by avenues of fruit trees or by orchards clustering around the villages and climbing the slopes.

With a total of 10.3 million inhabitants and an area of 30,449 square miles (78,864 sq km) the Czech Republic is one of the most densely populated countries in Europe. The greatest concentrations of people are around Prague, Plzeň (Pilsen) and Brno and in the industrial regions along the Ohře River in north Bohemia and around Ostrava, but towns and villages are scattered over the landscape.

Beginnings

In prehistoric times most of the land remained covered by the primeval forest which still survives today in pockets of the Šumava mountains. Only the warm and fertile valleys of the Labe and Morava were settled, by people who were skilled enough to fashion objects like the extraordinary 'Venus of Vestonice', a large-breasted and broad-hipped figurine made about 25,000 years ago. By the time the Romans were manning their frontier along the Danube, the Czech lands to the north, like much of Central and Western Europe, had been populated by Celts.

In the confused period which accompanied the decline of Roman power, the Czech lands were occupied first by Germanic groups and then, from the 6th century AD onwards, by new arrivals from the northeast, the Slavonic tribes who were the ancestors of the present Czechs, Moravians and Slovaks. For somewhat less than a century (AD833–906) a powerful political unit arose, the Great Moravian Empire (Velká Morava), bringing all these peoples together under unified rule and extending into present-day Hungary and Poland. The site of the imperial capital remains an enigma, though Moravians favour Staré Město, a suburb of Uherské Hradiště in the eastern part of the country. The short life of Velká Morava was brought to an end by the onrush of Hungarians from the east in AD907, not before the Moravians had brought in the Byzantine churchmen Cyril and Methodius to help consolidate Christianity; Cyril's name is immortalised in the Cyrillic script. Within the space of a century the Hungarians had been converted to Christianity, but their hold on Slovakia was to last a thousand years.

Kings, Emperors and a Turbulent Priest

Cut off from the east, Bohemia fell more and more into the German orbit. The Slavonic tribes who lived there were eventually dominated by one group, the Czechs, who gave it their own name (Čechy). Between the 9th and the 14th centuries it was ruled by the Premyslids. The legendary origin of this robust dynasty went back to Princess Libuše, a lady prone to visions. In the course of one trance she received a command to marry a ploughman named Přemysl, the ancestor of all subsequent rulers to bear that name.

The Přemyslids became Dukes, then Kings of a Bohemia which formed part of the essentially Germanic Holy Roman Empire. One of them was Václav (Wenceslas) I, who was canonised after his assassination by his brother Boleslav in 929 and became, together with his mother Ludmila, one of the country's patron saints. Later rulers such as Ottokar 1 (1198–1230) and Ottokar II (1253-78) invited large numbers of Germans into the country to found towns, develop crafts and industries, and to exploit the mineral wealth of the mountain ranges, as well as to settle in the previously uninhabited western borderlands. The splendour of the court at Prague owed much to the precious metals extracted from the ores of Jihlava and Kutná Hora. A peak of greatness was reached under the rule of Charles IV (1316–78), Holy Roman Emperor as well as King of Bohemia. In his reign the first university in Central Europe was founded, the Vltava was spanned by a splendid stone bridge, work began on the great Cathedral of St Vitus, and the streets and squares of Prague's New Town were laid out. More difficult times followed. Religious unrest, partly inspired by the teachings of the Englishman John Wycliffe, culminated in the burning of the charismatic preacher John Huss (Jan Hus) at the stake in Constance in 1415. The violent reaction to this betrayal (Huss had been given safe conduct to Constance to plead his case) included Prague's First Defenestration, when in 1419 his followers stormed Prague's Town Hall and threw a number of Catholic councillors from its windows. The Hussites founded the town of Tabor, south of Prague, ravaged the country far and wide, and defied the power of Pope and Emperor for many years before their eventual defeat at Lipany in 1434. This episode revealed a new national consciousness; Hus had preached in Czech; his adherents wanted a Czech national state, and much of their venom was directed against the Germans in the land, many of whom subsequently migrated to the border regions.

A Prague statue of Charles IV, King of Bohemia and Holy Roman Emperor

The Rule of the Habsburgs

At the beginning of the 16th century the Czech crown passed into the hands of the Habsburgs, some of whom chose to live in Prague, rather than Vienna.

The flame of Protestantism was readily kindled from the embers of Hussitism; by the start of the next century, most Czechs, including a majority of the nobility, were Lutherans. In 1618, enraged by the appointment of two Catholic governors, a band of Protestant aristocrats hurled the wretched pair and their secretary from a window of Hradčany Castle. This Second Defenestration precipitated the Thirty Years' War and the downfall of the Bohemian nobility and the Czech nation as a whole; the Protestant army was defeated in 1620 at Bilá Hora (White Mountain) just outside Prague, and many of Bohemia's leading Protestant aristocrats were executed in the Old Town Square, their severed heads subsequently stuck on spikes and displayed on the Charles Bridge. The more fortunate fled the land, their properties and their titles forfeited to Italian, Spanish and Austrian supporters of Pope and Emperor.

The Czechs were now a suppressed minority in their own land. The language of the country became German, while Czech was dismissed as the dialect of coachmen and washerwomen. The court took itself off to Vienna, and Prague became a sleepy provincial town. All forms of

Prague's dramatic castle gates

Protestantism were outlawed, and the Jesuits were brought in to enforce the ideals of the Counter-Reformation. Denied other forms of expression, the people's talents surged into music; Bohemian musicians manned many of the court bands maintained by German princelings, and Mozart was especially stimulated by the atmosphere of Prague, whose lovely Stavovské divadlo (Estates Theatre) was the venue for the première of his opera *Don Giovanni*.

Reawakening

By the beginning of the 19th century changes were stirring the Czech lands. It was in these provinces of the Habsburg empire that the Industrial Revolution took hold. Small-scale industries flourished in the borderlands, textile mills hummed in Brno, and the iron foundries of Ostrava marked the birth of one of Europe's great concentrations of heavy industry. Economic development was paralleled by the rebirth of national consciousness. The history of the Czechs was rediscovered (and idealised) by intellectuals like František Palacky. There was no thought at this stage of political independence, merely of encouraging the native culture and granting the lands of the Czech crown a status equal to that enjoyed by Hungary. The Habsburgs remained impervious to such pressures. In 1848, the Year of Revolutions, they missed their chance to reform their ramshackle realm, subduing Prague with a show of force and turning the reformist Reichsrat (national assembly) out of its temporary quarters in the Bishop's Palace at Kroměříž. In the decades that followed, the Czechs took every opportunity to strengthen their position against their German rivals. Much of the new industry was in the hands of German-speakers, while the migrant Czechs from the countryside supplied the labour. But soon industrial expansion had created a large new class of skilled workers, tradesmen, minor officials and schoolteachers, most of whom became passionate nationalists. Many places which had been German strongholds, like Brno or České Budějovice, were taken over by Czech-dominated councils. Prague, seemingly

Art Nouveau at its best in Prague's Obecní dům (Municipal House)

wholly German in 1800, had no more street signs in that language by the time of the outbreak of World War I.

An artistic renaissance accompanied these developments. National feeling permeates the music of Dvořák and Smetana, and found its architectural expression in bombastic classical buildings like Prague's National Museum (1890) and National Theatre (1883). By the turn of the century, Prague had become one of the great centres of Art Nouveau, known here as Secese (secession). This was a golden age of literature, too, much of it written in German by Prague's Jewish talents, such as Franz Kafka.

HISTORICAL AND ETHNIC MAP

A Republic of Our Own

World War I radicalised the Czechs. Forced to fight for the Habsburgs against their Russian cousins, they demurred; it was not unknown for whole regiments to desert to the Russians. By the end of the war, tens of thousands of Czech and Slovak legionaries were fighting on the Allied side, supplying useful backing for the politicians of this First Emigration, such as university professor and philosopher Tomas Garrigue Masaryk, his assistant Edvard Beneš and the Slovak scientist Milan Rastislav Štefánik, in their efforts to fashion a new post-war order. As Habsburg Austria-Hungary crumbled in late 1918, a new state of the Czechs and Slovaks arose; Czechoslovakia, proclaimed in Prague on 28 October, consisted of the lands of the Czech Crown, Bohemia, Moravia and part of Silesia, as well as Slovakia, and, in the far east of the new country, Ruthenia or Carpatho-Ukraine. Masaryk became the country's philosopher-President, a post he was to hold until his death in 1937.

This First Republic seemed to fulfil all the dreams of the Czechs: a state of their own, a liberal, parliamentary democracy, in which their language and culture were dominant. Its achievements were considerable; parliamentary democracy lasted until the end, social policy was progressive, backward Slovakia began to develop rapidly, and the country became one of the leading European centres of modernism in architecture and the arts. But the very structure of the state contained the faults which were to lead to its demise when Nazi Germany began to exert intolerable pressure in the late 1930s.

After the Czechs, the Germans formed the largest population group. Having ruled the roost under the Habsburgs, they had little love for the new dispensation, regarding it as a deliberate humiliation. Nevertheless, both sides were able for a while to use the state's democratic framework to arrive at acceptable compromises; German parties were represented in Parliament, German schools provided where needed, and so on.

The new state was highly centralised, with the centre of power firmly established in Prague.

As part of the 1,000-year-old Hungarian kingdom, Slovakia had been dominated by its Hungarian rulers; as Czechs flooded in to Slovakia to fill the professions which the Hungarians had vacated, many Slovaks felt that their old masters had simply been exchanged for new Czech ones. The promised autonomy for both Slovakia and the Sub-Carpathian Ukraine was never implemented.

Munich 1938

As the 1930s wore on, the allure of Nazism proved irresistible for many of Czechoslovakia's Germans. Abandoned in 1938 at Munich by her supposed allies, Britain and France, Czechoslovakia was forced to hand over the German-speaking Sudetenland to Hitler, the border area containing all her frontier defences and a large part of her industry. In March 1939, the leader of the Slovak separatists, the Catholic churchman Monsignor Tiso, was instructed by Hitler to declare independence. For a few short years the Slovaks had their own state, an achievement compromised by the activities of its own version of the SS, the Hlinka Guard, and by the delivery of its Jewish citizens to the death camps. As the state disintegrated,

Memorials to the victims of Nazi atrocities in Lidice

1938–45 BOUNDARY CHANGES

Ruthenia was grabbed by Hungary, a slice of Moravia by Poland. The German army marched through Prague; Hitler dined off Prague ham in Hradčany and greeted a carefully drilled German crowd from the castle window. Beneš, who had succeeded Masaryk as President, fled in despair; thousands of others, Slovaks as well as Czechs, joined him in the Second Emigration. Bohemia and Moravia became a Protectorate of the German Reich, its great armament factories and army equipment a bonus for the Wehrmacht, which drove into France a year later aboard Škoda tanks.
Based in London, Beneš laboured unceasingly for the reinstatement of his country, supported by many of his fellow-countrymen fighting in the uniforms of other nations. In 1942, disturbed by the lack of resistance at home, he sent parachutists to assassinate the acting Nazi Reichsprotektor Reinhard Heydrich. The Nazis' response was the execution of thousands and the destruction of the villages of Lidice and Ležáky. Czech resistance included systematic industrial sabotage, though armed resistance had to wait until the very last days of the war. In 1944 partisans and part of the Slovak army staged a national uprising, and for nearly two months, fierce fighting took place in central Slovakia. But the uprising was defeated, and both Slovakia and the Czech lands had to await liberation by the Red Army, though American troops under General Patton actually penetrated as far as Plzeň (Pilsen).

Back in triumph, and perhaps still smarting from the Western betrayal at Munich, Beneš orientated his policy towards the Soviet Union. The Communists, the biggest party in government, oversaw the expulsion of some 3 million Germans who had not been active opponents of Nazism.

Prague 1948
By February 1948, the Communists were able to squeeze out their democratic coalition partners. The decisive event was a huge rally addressed by Communist Prime Minister Gottwald in Prague's Old Town Square. Their *coup d'état* was eased by yet another defenestration, that of popular Foreign Minister Jan Masaryk, son of the former President, and the sole surviving non-Communist member of the government. Was his fall from the window of his flat in Prague's Cernín Palace suicide or murder? The question still awaits a wholly satisfactory answer.

There followed a totalitarian take-over in which no sphere of life was unaffected. Virtually every form of economic activity was nationalised, from steelworks to corner shops. Many fled the country; many were imprisoned, and potential opponents of the regime (such as members of the armed forces who had served in the West) were deprived of all possiblities of advancement. Eventually the revolution turned on its children; prominent Communists like Slánský went to the scaffold after 'confessing' to having been Western agents during a series of show trials.

Springtime and Autumn 1968
By the mid-1960s the Czech lands, which had inherited most of the wealth of Austria-Hungary, had a standard of living much lower than that of neighbouring Austria, a country with virtually no natural resources and little industry. Social and political pressures for reform could not be contained, and with the appointment of Alexander Dubček, as First Secretary of the Communist Party in early 1968, the 'Prague Spring' began. 'Socialism with a human face' became the declared aim of the government, and for a while the nation united enthusiastically

Jan Palach, who killed himself in protest at the Communist clampdown, remembered in Prague's Wenceslas Square

behind the regime. Brezhnev's Soviet Union and its allies feared, probably rightly, that the Czechoslovak Communist Party would be unable to contain the pressures for real change. While Czechs and Slovaks made the most of their first taste of freedom for 20 years, publishing pamphlets, founding political parties or simply crossing the border for a long-forbidden summer holiday, the Russians sent troops into Czechoslovakia for long-drawn out 'summer manœuvres'.

In the early hours of 21 August Russian tanks thundered across the borders. The government was arrested, flown to Moscow and forced to sign documents authorising the 'fraternal assistance' of its allies. Hope that at least some reforms might be preserved faded as leading figures of the short springtime were demoted, driven from office and deprived of their Party membership.

Paneláky – *Czech high-rise apartment blocks*

'Back to Normal'

Alexander Dubček was shunted aside, first as Ambassador to Turkey, then as a 'non-person', forced to live and work in obscurity as a clerk in the Forestry Commission in Bratislava. All forms of dissidence were ruthlessly stamped out by administrative measures such as dismissal from work or the exclusion of children from higher education.

The gloom which now descended on the country was deliberately relieved by an attempt to satisfy material needs. Shop shelves were filled with goods, though admittedly not in great variety and not always of the highest quality. The number of private cars increased dramatically, and the masses (some at least) were housed in *paneláky*, the high-rise system-built apartment blocks which dominate the approach to virtually every town. The cult of the second home reached almost fantastic proportions; it was rare for a middle-class family not to have their *chata* (chalet) on the edge of town or in the depths of the countryside.

A Velvet Revolution

Not everyone was prepared to accept arbitrary rule softened by a semi-satisfactory standard of

living. In 1977 a group of intellectuals, foremost among them the playwright Václav Havel, signed Charter 77, a document demanding that the government respect the human rights guaranteed by the country's constitution. The demand was met with harassment of all kinds; writers and university lecturers who had signed the charter suddenly found themselves working as lorry drivers or stokers, while Havel himself was shifting barrels in a brewery, when not actually in prison.

Confident in its ability to keep dissidents firmly in check, the regime seemed unconcerned by the changes which followed Soviet President Gorbachev's launch of *perestroika* in the mid-1980s. Its own adoption of *přestavba* was more of a token gesture than a sincere attempt at reform. But as the Communist house of cards collapsed in 1989, even this most rigid of regimes could not remain unaffected. On 17 November, an officially approved demonstration marking the Nazis' suppression of the Czech universities turned into a protest march which was viciously put down by riot police. The event acted as a catalyst; striking students were joined by actors, and colleges and theatres all over the country became the focus of popular protest, which soon spread to the factory workers. In Prague, Charter 77 joined with other groups to form Občanské Forum (Civic Forum), with Havel at its head, and a parallel evolution took place in Bratislava under the heading of VPN (Public Against Violence). Huge demonstrations took place, one in Wenceslas Square addressed by both Havel and Alexander Dubček, whisked back from obscurity in Bratislava. The regime's impotence was exposed, and by 10 December a new government had been formed in which Communists formed a minority. On 29 December Václav Havel was installed as President of the Republic in the Vladislav Hall on the Hradčany heights.

Into the Unknown

Havel was confirmed as President in free elections in July 1990. The official title of the country he headed had become the Czech and Slovak Federative Republic, a name agreed

BACKGROUND

Třeboň, in South Bohemia

only after long haggling, as Slovaks sought the greatest possible degree of autonomy. The years which followed the Velvet Revolution were dominated by concern with the disastrous state of the economy on the one hand and by Czech-Slovak tension on the other.

The problem of an economy which produced goods 'of no interest to anyone, while we are lacking the things we need' (Havel's first New Year address to the nation) may well take decades to solve. The mining, steel and chemicals industries had undergone forced growth under Communism, regardless of their impact on the environment, and the economy as a whole was tied to the Soviet Union, which supplied cheap raw materials. This link has now been severed, and a dash is under way in the Czech Republic to create a viable market economy by privatisation of enterprises of all kinds, from shops (the 'Little Privatisation') to large-scale industry ('Big Privatisation'), with membership of the European Community as a medium-term aim. Western capital is actively encouraged by means of joint ventures, like the tie-up between Volkswagen and Škoda. The closure of plants turning out goods no-one wants has led to a sharp increase in

unemployment; the creation of new enterprises is the intended solution.

Under Communism, the country had been a nominally federal state, with Czech and Slovak parliaments as well as a national assembly. After 1989 Slovak politicians played the nationalist card, fanning long-standing resentment of the Czechs into demands not just for autonomy but for full sovereignty. The elections of 1992 sharpened differences between the two halves of the country; in the Czech lands, the avowedly Thatcherite free-marketeer Václav Klaus gathered most votes, while in Slovakia the robust populist Vladimir Mečiar, ex-Communist turned nationalist, was the clear winner. Unable or unwilling to compromise, each found the break-up of the country the easiest way to implement his political programme. Ignoring President Havel's advice and refusing to hold a referendum, they agreed to differ, and at midnight on 31 December 1992 Czechoslovakia ceased to exist, replaced by the independent Czech and Slovak Republics. A tragic harbinger of the separation had been the death, shortly before, of the symbol of hopeful nationhood, Alexander Dubček.

What to See

The essential rating system:

✓	'top ten'

◆◆◆   do not miss
◆◆   see if you can
◆   worth seeing if you
         have time

Most visitors to the Czech Republic head for Prague, and rightly so. The hundred-spired city has attractions enough to fill far more than a single holiday. But it would be a mistake only to see Prague, or even to make it the sole base for excursions, although there is any number of fascinating day trips to be made from the capital, to castles at Konopiště and Karlštejn, to Lidice and Terezín with their sombre memories, or simply to enjoy the natural delights of the wooded valleys of the Berounka and Sazava Rivers.

The country's grandest scenery is concentrated in the wooded uplands that it shares with its neighbours Poland, Germany and Austria. The highest summits, and also the most popular, are to be found in the north and northeast, in the Giant Mountains and in the Jeseníky Mountains of Moravia. The Ore Mountains of northern Bohemia are the most affected by acid rain, while the southwestern Šumava, along the border with

Architectural elegance: the magnificent Karlův most (Charles Bridge) in Prague

Bavaria, is perfect for walking in solitude. Intriguing rock formations appropriately known as the Czech Paradise or Czech Switzerland attract many visitors, as do the spectacular caves of the Moravian Karst, near Brno. Less spectacular, but equally rewarding, are the harmonious landscapes of south Bohemia, studded by countless great ponds, in which swim the carp destined to become part of the country's traditional Christmas dinner.

No other Czech city has quite the allure of Prague, but all the larger places have a strong identity of their own and something special to show the visitor. As the capital of Moravia, lively Brno is not ashamed to mix its historical heritage with an up-to-date approach to life, while its rival, ancient Olomouc, boasts more listed buildings than anywhere outside Prague. In the northwest, the famous Bohemian Triangle of sophisticated spa towns led by Karlovy Vary (Carlsbad) attracts not just those in search of a cure, but many others who appreciate their elegance and

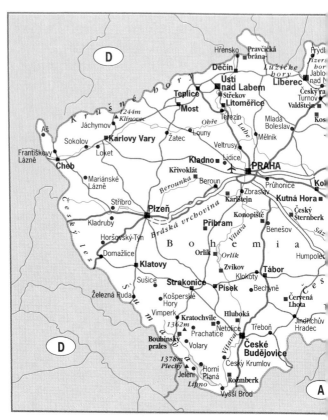

relaxed pace. But the real wealth of both Bohemia and Moravia is in the constellation of smaller towns. No-one should miss Český Krumlov in southern Bohemia or Telč in southern Moravia, and in virtually every part of the country you will find some little treasure of a place, not always in a pristine state of repair, but invariably rewarding.

Sometimes tucked away in the town, sometimes hiding in the forest or dominating a dramatic river valley are innumerable castles and country seats – more per square kilometre here than in most other countries. These cover a wide range of periods and styles, from rambling fortress-cum-palaces, built and rebuilt over the centuries, like the great pile

THE CZECH REPUBLIC

...verlooking Krumlov, to elegant ...nd impeccably planned ...aroque edifices like Slavkov ...r secluded moated manors ...ach as Červená Lhota. ...espite the fact that the Czech ...nd Slovak Republics have now ...stablished themselves as ...eparate and sovereign states, ...ey will continue to ...omplement each other in ...any ways. Travellers to this area certainly should not rule out an itinerary which allows for a visit to both states. For any visitor to the Czech Republic it is well worth considering a journey to Slovakia's Danube capital, Bratislava, or perhaps planning a visit to that classic contrast to the peaceful Czech countryside – the wild peaks of the High Tatras mountains, far away to the east.

PRAGUE (PRAHA) ✓

For many of its admirers, Prague, *matka měst* ('mother of cities'), has all the ingredients of the perfect metropolis. It is large (with a population of over a million), but not so large that it cannot be grasped in its entirety; it has kept its extraordinarily rich heritage of historic buildings and townscape intact like no other European capital. World War II left the physical fabric of Prague largely untouched; few bombs fell on the city and in May 1945 it fell swiftly to the Resistance and the Red Army. The following 40 years of freedom from commercial pressures

PRAGUE (PRAHA)

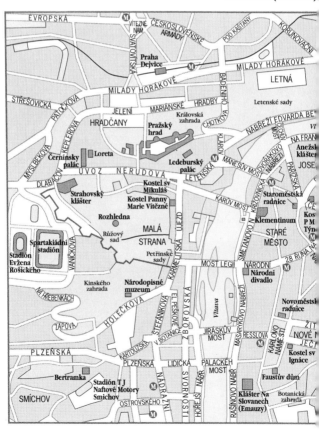

staved off the redevelopment which has now destroyed the harmony of most other European cities.

Above the roofs rise a hundred towers and steeples, unaccompanied by ungainly office blocks or high-rise flats. Buildings of every era stand side by side, from the burgher's house to baroque palace, from Art Nouveau apartment block to Cubist café. At ground level, the streets and alleyways laid out in the Middle Ages are full of crowds going about their business, along with growing numbers of visitors and tourists. The worst effects of traffic are kept at bay by trams and the Metro, as well as by pedestrianisation; more than most, this city is one to walk and loiter in. At every turn, new visual delights present themselves, from baroque house signs to the sudden and exhilerating sight of the castle as you escape from the confines of the Old Town to the riverside. Prague has several historic cores. High up above the broad Vltava is the castle complex, Hradčany, incorporating one of the continent's great Gothic cathedrals. Terraced gardens step down to the delightfully intimate Malá Strana (Lesser Town), somehow fitted in between castle and river. Karluv most (Charles Bridge), Europe's longest and most beautiful medieval bridge, leads to the Staré Město (Old Town) whose maze of narrow streets is centred on its cobbled square and on the poignant remains of Josefov, the old Ghetto. The medieval Nové Město (New Town) has as its main axis the world-famous square which is really a boulevard, tree-lined Václavské náměstí (Wenceslas Square).

◆◆◆
HRADČANY

A hilltop cathedral town rather than just a castle, Prague's Hradčany is the symbolic heart of the nation. The easily defended rock spur which

Stromovka
HOLEŠOVICE
ELETRŽNÍ
DY HORÁKOVÉ
Praha Bubny
odní
hnické
zeum
BUBENSKÁ
DUKELSKÝCH HRDINŮ
ARGENTINSKÁ
ENSKÝ
UNEL
NÁBŘEŽÍ EDVARDA BENEŠE
HLÁVKŮV MOST
Zimní stadión
Ostrov Štvanice
TĚSNOVSKÝ TUNEL
Poštovní muzeum
Muzeum hlavního města Prahy
WILSONOVA
SOKOLOVSKÁ
KŘIŽÍKOVA
NA PORÍČÍ
Praha Masarykovo nádraží
Hudební divadlo v Karlíně
TROCNÓVSKÁ
HYBERNSKÁ
HUSITSKÁ
HUSITSKÁ
SEIFERTOVA
WILSONOVA
SEVONOVA
Praha-hlavní nádraží
ITALSKÁ
árodní uzeum
Riegrovy sady
VINOHRADSKÁ
ITALSKÁ
NGLICKÁ
Kostel Nejsv Srdce Páně
SLAVÍKOVA
VINOHRADY
SLAVSKÁ
NÁMĚSTÍ MÍRU
VINOHRADSKÁ
SLEZSKÁ
NSKÁ
KORUNNÍ
HRADSKA
FRANCOUZSKÁ
0   300   600 m

forces the Vltava into a great eastward bend was first fortified towards the end of the 9th century by the founder of the Přemyslid dynasty, Prince Bořivoj. The royal palace, together with a church, the second to be built in Bohemia, was the predecessor of the great complex of ecclesiastical and governmental buildings of all periods which stretches along the ridge today, stepping down to Malá Strana through glorious terraced gardens, cut off from the plateau to the north by a deep moat. Seen from below, the soaring Gothic outline of St Vitus' Cathedral is held firmly in place by the endlessly elongated, implacable façade of the palace buildings.

The Hrad (Castle)

The castle can be approached in a number of ways: from Malostranská Metro station via Staré zámecké schody (Old Castle Steps); from Malostranské náměstí via Zámecké schody (Castle Steps) or via Nerudová and the hairpin bend of Ke zámku, or from the north across the Powder Bridge. The most dramatic entrance is from Hradčanské náměstí. The castle's front door, the First Courtyard, is watched over by battling stone giants and by the palace guards in their less than intimidating blue uniforms, designed by a friend of President Havel. The Changing of the Guard is now a cheerful affair rather than the sombre display of state power carried out by the goose-stepping khaki-clad figures of the previous regime. Beyond the baroque Matthias Gate (which once marked the castle's western extremity), the Second Courtyard was given its present appearance (like much of the rest of the castle) in the course of the 18th century. In the centre is a fountain, to the south a chapel and to the north the castle's gallery, housing an idiosyncratic collection of paintings amassed by Emperor Rudolph II.

The castle's Third Courtyard, with a delicate statue of St George and the Dragon, is dominated by **St Vitus' Cathedral**, a great structure whose construction was spread over the centuries, though its spirit remains entirely Gothic. Its unique outline owes not a little to the wonderful way in which its tall tower was capped in Renaissance and baroque times. The cathedral was commissioned in 1344 by Charles IV to replace the Romanesque basilica which itself had been built over a round church of the early 10th century. In charge of the early work was one of the greatest architects of Gothic Europe, Peter Parler, whose inspired hand can been seen in the Golden Gate or South Door, and the vaulting of the east end. Parlér also built **St Wenceslas' Chapel**, into the door of which is set the Romanesque knocker to which the saint is supposed to have clung as he was murdered on the orders of his brother Boleslav. Seven locks secure the door to the chamber in which the crown jewels of Bohemia are kept. The cathedral is a treasure-house of tombs, the most spectacular baroque example being that of St John of Nepomuk in the ambulatory. The building of the cathedral was brought to a triumphant conclusion in the late 19th and early 20th century, when the interior was adorned with fine stained glass from designs by eminent Czech artists like Max Švabinsky and Alfons Mucha.

The southeastern corner of the Third Courtyard is formed by the **Royal Palace**, a complex structure in itself, for centuries the home of Bohemian kings. Its most spectacular interior space is the astonishing Vladislav Hall, a vast room whose early Renaissance windows contrast with the writhing tracery of its vaulting, a last gasp of Gothic inventiveness by its designer, Benedikt Ried. Ried was also responsible for the equally imaginative Riders Staircase. A terrace gives a regal panorama over the city, and you can also visit the room which was the scene of the Second Prague Defenestration in 1618.

The east end of the cathedral faces **St George's Basilica**, whose baroque west front conceals the much-restored Romanesque building; its antiquity is hinted at by the twin towers in pale stone at its eastern end. The adjoining convent houses the National Gallery's **Czech Art Collection**, with paintings ranging in date from the Middle Ages to the 18th century.

The castle's streets outdo in fascinating detail the rather bland façades of its three

St John of Nepomuk's tomb, St Vitus

courtyards. Jiřská (George Street) has fine buildings like the Lobkowicz Palace (with a museum of Czech history), and an alleyway off Vikarská leads to the Mihulka, a tower forming part of the northern fortifications. Most intriguing of all is Zlatá ulička (Golden Lane), whose miniature dwellings, now turned into souvenir shops, were once the abode of goldsmiths. At its far end stands the Daliborka, a 15th-century round tower.

Outside the walls to the north, reached via the Powder Bridge, are further buildings connected to the castle's history. The Riding School, to the left, houses a gallery, and the Royal Gardens, to the right, eventually lead to one of the city's most charming buildings, the **Royal Summer Palace** or Belvedere of 1569. With its graceful arcade and curving copper roof, and overlooking an intimate formal garden graced by a 'singing fountain', it seems to have been spirited here in one piece from early Renaissance Italy.

While the crowds lean over the parapet transfixed by the panorama of Prague, the castle guards outside the First Courtyard stare impassively westwards up the gently sloping Hradčanské náměstí (Hradčany Square), lined with palaces. The ornately sgraffitoed Schwarzenberg Palace now houses a **Military History Museum** filled with the

Loreta cloisters

fearsome but often elegant weaponry of pre-World War I battles, while the sumptuous (and only occasionally open) Archbishop's Palace, opposite, proclaims the (often contested) power of the Church. Tucked away is the Sternberk Palace, now part of the National Gallery, whose Collection of European Art is the country's finest.

Of the dozens of copies made of the Virgin Mary's house miraculously transported from the Holy Land to Loreto in Italy, the Prague **Loreta** has the most sumptuous setting of all. The fanciful façade of the baroque complex is the work of the Dietzenhofers, topped by a tower housing the ultimate in musical boxes, a carillon which plays the hymn *A Thousand Times We Greet Thee*. Opposite this exercise in joyous frivolity created by the church stands the much more serious **Černínsky palac (Černín Palace)**, with a massively colonnaded façade. Begun in 1669 for Count Černín, the Imperial ambassador to Venice this seemed an altogether appropriate home for the newly-created Czechoslovak Foreign Ministry in 1918. Its sombre air seems justified when it is recalled that it was here in the dark days of early 1948 that the most recent Prague defenestration took place, that of Jan Masaryk. Entered by its baroque gateway, **Strahovský Klášter (Strahov Monastery)** was founded around 1140, but its present appearance, including the twin towers visible from afar, is the result of rebuilding a

Malá Strana seen from the Hrad

he end of the 17th century. It owes its main attraction, its magnificent libraries, to the misfortunes of other monasteries, whose collections, confiscated by the Emperor in the 1780s and the Communists in the 1940s and '50s, found a home here in the richly decorated Theological and Philosophical Halls. Books, manuscripts and antique globes compete for attention with intricately carved bookcases and painted ceilings. Strahov is also the Museum of Czech Literature.

◆◆◆
MALÁ STRANA

Whether translated as Little Quarter or Lesser Town, the name of Prague's Malá Strana seems to imply a humble part of the city, crouching at the foot of the castle hill and hemmed in by the Vltava. It's certainly the most picturesque part of

Prague, its houses, palaces and churches packed in tightly along the sometimes steeply sloping streets, pan-tiled roofs alternating with the greenery of walled and terraced gardens, and an almost rustic feeling where trees overhang the riverbank and orchards climb up towards the Petřín Hill. Malá Strana's origins go back beyond its formal foundation by King Ottokar II in 1257 to a scatter of buildings around a market. Around 1360 it was extended and given new fortifications – the Hunger Wall, which still runs up the hillside today. Much rebuilding took place in the aftermath of the Thirty Years' War, when many of the those on the winning side ensconced themselves in the marvellous baroque palaces which are nowadays used to house embassies.

Linking the Old Town with Malá Strana is **Karlův most (Charles Bridge)**, whose 16 Gothic arches carry it on a gently curving alignment from the bridgehead towers at either end, accompanied by a procession of theatrically gesticulating stone saints. It was begun in 1357 in the reign of Emperor Charles IV, the definitive replacement for previous bridges destroyed by floods. Now given over to strollers and idlers and those trying to sell them something, it is difficult to imagine the days when it was the only river crossing, traversed until the 1950s by a tram line. But it was always more than a mere traffic route; executions took place here, the most famous being that of St John Nepomuk, thrown from the parapet to drown in 1393. Now the patron saint of bridges, he is commemorated on river crossings all over Central Europe, most notably here, in bronze, in the middle of the north parapet.

Steps lead down from the bridge to tranquil **Kampa** island, cut off from Malá Strana by the millstream known as Čertovká (The Devil's Brook), where mill-wheels turned until the 1930s. Two towers guard the western bridgehead, the stockier southern one dating back to the days of the first, wooden bridge, the northern one worth climbing for the view from its gallery. Ahead rises a glorious skyline whose dominant feature is the splendid dome of St Nicholas Church, built between 1702 and 1753 by the Dientzenhofer architectural dynasty, with an interior of unrivalled sumptuousness. The great baroque church almost overwhelms the Lesser Town's focal point, **Malostranské náměstí (Malá Strana Square)**, with its busy tram stop and shops in a varied framework of ancient town houses and grand palaces such as the Liechtensteins'. Most visitors make off up **Nerudová**, the cobbled street rising to the west, named after the 19th-century writer Jan Neruda, and lined with fine old houses, many with splendid doorways and house signs. Running parallel is Vlašská, leading to the palaces of the Schönborns and the Lobkovices, which now house the US and German embassies respectively. To the south, between traffic-choked Karmelitská and the river, is a network of intimate streets and squares, while to the north is the **Valdštejn Palace**, the great urban residence built for himself by Albrecht von Wallenstein, the over-ambitious Imperial commander of the Thirty Years' War; its walled garden is a wonderful refuge, with a great arched *sala terrena* an extraordinary tufa grotto and a riding school, now part of the National Gallery.

◆◆◆
NOVÉ MĚSTO

Six and a half centuries old, Prague's extensive New Town was laid out by King Charles IV in the middle of the 14th century as a carefully planned extension to the city. Its relatively spacious streets and squares are in dramatic contrast to the labyrinthine Old Town, which is embraced by two of its important arteries, **Na příkopě (Moat Street)**, and **Narodní třída**, laid out along the line of old fortifications. Together with **Václavské náměstí (Wenceslas Square)**, running gently uphill to the National Museum, they make up the modern core of the city, with shops and banks, hotels and cafés, theatres and cinemas. Wenceslas Square is actually a tree-lined, partly traffic-free boulevard. Once known as the Horse Market, it is the theatre where much recent history has been acted out, from the declaration of the Republic in 1918 to the triumphant balcony appearance of Václav Havel and Alexander Dubček during the Velvet Revolution of 1989. The bronze statue of the good king dates from 1913; this is where Jan Palach burnt himself to death in 1969 in protest

against the Russian invasion of the previous year. No high-rises mar the architectural unity of the square; most of its buildings are early to mid-20th century in date, ranging from the austere modernism of the Bata store to the flamboyant Art Nouveau of the Hotel Evropa. A more dominant site could hardly have been found for the **Národní muzeum (National Museum)**, its architecture an overpowering monument to 19th-century Czech nationalism, its equally grandiose interior a pompous setting for interminable archæological, natural historical and cultural collections. The Magistral, its impact equivalent to an urban motorway, cuts off the Museum, then heads north past the grotesque Parliament Building of the 1970s, the 19th-century Opera (Smetana Theatre), and the wonderful Art Nouveau

Sculpture in the Národní muzeum

Central Station building of 1908. Leading eastwards from the foot of Wenceslas Square and lined with buildings of similar character is pedestrianised **Na příkopě**, which leads into Náměstí Republiky (Republic Square). Next to the Powder Tower stands perhaps the most extraordinary Art Nouveau structure in the city; the **Obecní dům (Municipal House)**, completed in 1911, was the outcome of the collaborative work of many of the major artists and designers of the period, and houses cafés, a restaurant, exhibition and performance halls. An older Prague is evoked beyond the motorway viaduct to the east in the **City Museum**, whose prize exhibit is a wonderful early 19th-century model of Prague. Further Art Nouveau glamour is evident in two famous façades adjoining each other along Narodní třída, at the opposite end of Na příkopě to Náměstí Republiky – the Topic publishers and the Prague Insurance Co – but the high point of the boulevard comes where it meets the river. Here stands the monumental **Národní divadlo (National Theatre)**, erected in 1881 from funds contributed by patriotic Czechs, who paid out again when the place burned down within weeks of opening. The recent extension is more controversial, but is so far intact.

The New Town extends far to the south in the direction of Vyšehrad, its riverside magnificently defined by an almost continuous cliff of 19th- and early 20th-century façades;

behind one of them is the private residence of President Havel. Among the often grim apartment blocks stretching inland is **Karlovo náměstí (Charles Square)**, its trees making it more of a park than a square. Resslová ulice leads down towards the river, passing on its way the **Kostel Sv Cyrila a Metodeje (Church of Cyril and Methodius)**, in whose crypt perished the parachutists sent from England to assassinate Nazi Reichsprotektor Heydrich. A few blocks to the east of Charles Square, on Ke Karlovu, is the Vila Amerika, a wonderful little baroque villa which now houses the **Dvořák Museum**. Just around the corner from here is another sort of shrine, **U Kalicha (The Flagon)**, the pub where in 1914 Hasek's fictional creation, the Good Soldier Švejk, was shopped to the Austrian secret police.

◆◆◆
STARÉ MESTO (OLD TOWN)

Within the girdle of broad streets which run where walls and moats once stood is a closely meshed web of streets and alleyways, the ancient Prague of mayors and merchants and the civic counterpoise to the feudal stronghold of Hradcany, on its rock beyond the river.

The Old Town focuses on its cobbled square, **Staroměstské náměstí**, an irregular space defying all the rules of logical town planning. Almost always cheerfully crowded with tourists and entertainers, the square is lined with grand town houses

The Huss Monument, Staré Mesto

and even grander palaces; it's overlooked to the north by the baroque **Svatý Mikulás (Church of St Nicholas)** and dominated by the **Staroměstská radnice (Old Town Hall)**. Here the crowds gather to watch the circling figures set in motion by the intricate medieval mechanism of the Astronomical Clock. Death opens the performance; Turk and Jew, Vice and Virtue nod and dance, and a cockerel closes the display. The Old Town Hall was badly damaged during the Prague Uprising in May 1945, but you can tour the interior, then climb to the top of the tall tower for one of the best views of the city. The focal point of the square, and of much Czech sentiment, is the astonishing Art

Nouveau sculpture making up the **Huss Monument**. The Goltz-Kinsky Palace has one of the city's finest rococo façades, while over the Gothic building known as the House of the Stone Bell and its gabled neighbours rise the impressive, almost sinister towers, spires and spikes of the **Tyn Church**. Threading its way through the Old Town is the **Royal Way**, the processional pathway followed by the monarch at his coronation. It begins at the late Gothic **Prasná brána (Powder Tower)** defending the junction of Old and New Towns in the east (climb its winding staircase for another wonderful view), then follows the baroque and

Gravestones are crowded together in the Old Jewish Cemetery

rococo façades of **Celetná ulice**, passing through the Old Town Square and wriggling its way westward through little streets and squares until it reaches the cluster of towers and churches guarding the Old Town end of the Charles Bridge. Use this as an axis for exploring the maze of streets and alleyways to the south, full of treasures like the **Stavovské divadlo (Estates Theatre)**, where Mozart premiered *Don Giovanni* in 1787, or the **Bethlehem Chapel**, where Jan Hus once preached. One of the finest views in Prague can be enjoyed from the waterfront near the neo-Renaissance **Smetana Museum**.

North of the Old Town Square stretches what once was Prague's Ghetto, given the name Josefov in honour of tolerant and liberalising Emperor Joseph II. The Jews had lived in Prague since the 10th century; by the middle of the 19th, many had become assimilated and moved out to more salubrious quarters, and the old Ghetto had become a sink of overcrowding, poverty and disease. The authorities' answer was to redevelop it, replacing the warren of streets with a grand turn-of-the-century Parisian-style boulevard, **Pařížská**, but a number of key buildings still stand. Several synagogues serve as museums, but the **Staronová synagoga (Old-New Synagogue)**, one of the most venerable Gothic buildings in the city is still functioning as such, while the Jewish Town Hall houses a kosher restaurant. The most moving area is the **Starý židovský hrbitov (Old Jewish Cemetery)**, its dead buried 12-deep amid a chaos of tombstones, one of which recalls wise Rabbi Loew, who breathed life into clay to make that figure of Prague legend, the Golem. Backing on to the cemetery is one of the city's most fascinating but frustrating museums, the **Uměleckoprůmyslové muzeum (Decorative Arts Museum)**, with only limited space to display its wealth of objects from every era. Pařížská heads north towards the vacant plinth topping the heights on the far side of the Svatopluk Čech Bridge, where the monstrous Stalin statue once stood. Downstream from the modern Intercontinental Hotel is **Anežský klášter (St Agnes' Convent)**, immaculately restored and now housing a selection of some of the best of the 19th-century Czech paintings from the collections of the National Gallery.

Other Sights

BERTRAMKA (MOZART MUSUEM)

Mozartová 169, Smíchov
Mozart stayed here with his friends, the Dušeks, on a number of occasions, most notably when rushing his opera *Don Giovanni* to completion by candlelight before its premiere. Furnishings include his harpsichord and piano.

LETNÁ PLAIN

The Hradčany heights are continued eastwards by this vast open plateau, once the site of May Day demonstrations. Its southern rim is formed by landscaped spaces descending steeply to the Vltava. The giant statue of Stalin stood here briefly, from 1955 to 1962, when it was blown up. Its vacant plinth gives a fine view down Pařížská on the far side of the river into the Old Town. Two establishments profit from the view: the extravagantly Art Nouveau café to the west, the steel and glass restaurant pavilion from the Brussels Expo of 1956 to the east. Near the latter is the **Národní technické muzeum (National Technical Museum)**, showing cars, trains, planes and much else besides.

PETŘÍN HILL

The wooded slopes to the west of Malá Strana lead up to one of the city's most spectacular viewpoints, the 197-foot (60m)-high 'Eiffel Tower' crowning Petřín Hill, a relic of the Prague Industrial Exhibition of 1891.

TROJA

Thousands head out to this northeastern suburb at weekends for its zoo, but in 1679 Count Šternberk chose what was then a pleasantly countrified setting for his splendid **Trojský zámek (Troja Palace)**. Designed by a French architect, and recently restored, it has a formal garden, a superb banqueting hall and stone giants fighting it out around the balustrades and stairways outside.

VYŠEHRAD

It was here that the legendary Princess Libuše foresaw the founding of Prague, and Vyšehrad (High Castle) has suffered many vicissitudes since it formed an alternative royal residence to Hradčany in the 10th and 11th centuries. Charles IV favoured it as a starting point for the coronation procession; the Hussites destroyed what they could of it, while the Habsburgs cleared its occupants out and refortified it to keep an eye on the potentially unruly city. In the late 19th century Vyšehrad became the focus of nationalist feeling; it was here that the **National Cemetery** was sited, where great Czechs lie honoured. Some 50 of them are buried in the Pantheon or Slavín. Vyšehrad is a curious medley of features, including the much-restored Church of St Peter and St Paul, the round Church of St Martin, and remains of baroque fortifications. Its views over city and river are outstanding.

EXCURSIONS FROM PRAGUE

Southeast

KONOPIŠTĚ CASTLE

Near Benešov, 25 miles (40km) southeast of Prague via D1 and Tabor Highway 3

Like Pruhonice, the ancient castle at Konopiště was remodelled towards the end of the 19th century in order to conform more closely to that age's idea of what a medieval stronghold should look like. At the same time it was given the strictly un-medieval setting of a landscape park laid out in the English style. The person who was responsible for these improvements was the heir to the Austro-Hungarian throne, Habsburg Archduke Franz Ferdinand (see below). The Archduke was an avid huntsman, who was himself destined to be hunted down, with devastating and far-reaching consequences, by a Serbian nationalist at Sarajevo on a fateful day in June 1914.

◆
PRUHONICE PARK

10 miles (16km) southeast via Brno motorway (D1)

The collection of trees and shrubs assembled by Emperor Franz Josef's aristocratic Minister of Agriculture is one of the richest in Central Europe, laid out among the lakes and garden pavilions of an extensive English-style landscape park. Pruhonice Castle dates back to the Middle Ages, but was rebuilt in neo-Gothic style at the end of the 19th century at the same time as the park was created.

South

Pleasant river scenery can be enjoyed not only along the Vltava, but also in the wooded valley of its tributary, the Sázava, a favourite setting for weekend walks and second homes. The Vltava has been dammed at a number of points to generate hydro-electric power, turning it into a series of linear lakes (Slapy, Orlík),

---

An obsessive Archduke

When not travelling round the world, or trying to preserve the soon-to-be-extinguished monarchy, Franz Ferdinand spent much of his time at Konopiste with his beloved wife, Sophie Chotek, daughter of an old Moravian aristocratic family, whom he had married despite the fierce opposition of the Imperial court. Just before the outbreak of World War I the castle was the scene of a secret meeting with Kaiser Wilhelm II of Germany. The Archduke's obsessions are very evident here, most depressingly in the endless array of hunting trophies; the toll of creatures foolish enough to stray within range of his gun runs into six figures. There are plenty of arms and armour displayed here, as well as an odd collection of St George memorabilia. Outside, the park and a rose garden come as a welcome relief from these preoccupations of another century.

which may have diminished its natural beauty but makes it a very attractive setting for watersports of all kinds.

◆
ORLÍK
46 miles (75km) south via Highways 4 and 19
Here the valley has been flooded for a length of more than 37 miles (60km), creating a new setting for the castles of Orlík and Zvikov, rising above the widened river. **Orlík Castle**, a property of the Schwarzenbergs, suffered neo-Gothic restoration in the 19th century. Its interior is elaborately furnished. By contrast, **Zvikov Castle** retains its authentic medieval air, its

round tower looming in an almost extravagantly picturesque way over the cliffs and forest at the point where the Otava joins the Vltava. It has a superb arcaded courtyard and a Royal Chapel with wall-paintings and a fine altarpiece.

◆
ZBRASLAV
7 miles (12km) south via Příban Highway 4
A favourite spot for city excursions by steamer, riverside Zbraslav has an ancient monastery whose internal spaces and grounds now make a calm and elegant setting for the fascinating 19th- and 20th-century **Czech Sculpture Collection** of the National Gallery.

Konopiště Castle

Southwest

KARLŠTEJN CASTLE

*17 miles (28km) southwest via
Highways 4, 115 and 116; by
train from Prague-Smíchov
(Smíchovské nadráží)*

With its towers and battlements
rising proudly over the
attractive wooded valley of the
Berounka River, this is the most
visited of all the castles of the
Bohemian countryside, built in
the mid-14th century by
Emperor Charles IV both as a
retreat and as a secure place
for the crown jewels and other
precious relics of the Holy
Roman Empire.

Even the Hussites were put off
by the long climb up to the
castle from the valley bottom,
and went away after laying
siege to it for seven months. By
then the castle's treasure had
gone anyway; the regalia of the
Bohemian Crown eventually
ended up in the Prague
Cathedral, the Imperial insignia
in Vienna. The rebuilding
carried out at the time of the
Renaissance was reversed by
the restoration which took place
between 1887 and 1899, and
Karlštejn owes its present
appearance almost entirely to
19th-century conceptions of
how a medieval stronghold
should look. Authenticity is not
the strong point, but it still
impresses, more by its romantic
silhouette than by its heavily
restored interiors. The most
moving of these is Charles' tiny
Chapel of St Catherine, all
gilded plaster and semi-
precious stones. Opening times
may vary during restoration.

KŘIVOKLÁT CASTLE

*27 miles (44km) west of Prague
via Highways 6 and 201*

Near the confluence of the
winding Berounka with one of
its tributaries stands another
one of Bohemia's royal castles,
less heavily subjected to the
restorer's hand than Karlštejn.
Křivoklát goes back to the 11th
century; in Charles IV's time it
served as a royal hunting lodge.
Its most prominent feature is the
tall round tower rising over the
woodland of the Křivoklátská
Vrchovina (Křivoklát Uplands),
but it is also remarkable for its
Gothic chapel, which has an
exceptionally fine altarpiece.

North

LIDICE

*15 miles (24km) northwest via
Highways 7 and 551*

On 10 June 1942, the male
population of the mining village
of Lidice was massacred by the
SS and Gestapo, and the
women sent to a concentration
camp together with their
children (save for those thought
capable of being
'Germanised'). The village was
then razed to the ground, and
its name erased from the
record, all in indiscriminate
revenge for the assassination of
acting Reichsprotektor
Heydrich by Czechoslovak
parachutists sent from England.
Under the slogan 'Lidice Shall
Live' the village was rebuilt
after the war, a symbol of
endurance and continuity. Next
to it, the site of old Lidice is a
shrine, with cross, memorial

and museum, and foundations of some of the original buildings.

A survivor of the Lidice massacre

◆
MĚLNÍK
22 miles (36km) north via Highway 9
The castle town of Mělník, overlooking the confluence of the Vltava and the Labe, is an ancient place, first fortified in the 9th century. Here Queen Ludmila brought up her grandson, later to become St Wenceslas. When Emperor Charles IV added the crown of Burgundy to his list of titles he brought vines and vintners from his new domain, and ever since then Mělník has been the centre of the (not very extensive) wine-growing area of Bohemia. The vines covering the steep slope between castle and river add greatly to its appeal. The town has kept one of its old gateways and its arcaded marketplace, while the castle houses a wine museum, a gallery and a restaurant, which makes the

most of its strategic location high up above the river.

East

◆◆
KUTNÁ HORA
43 miles (69km) east via Highway 12
The great days of what is now a medium-sized provincial town began in the 13th century, when abundant deposits of silver ore were discovered. Prospectors swarmed in, a mint was founded, grand private houses were built and fine churches were constructed, the greatest of them being the **Church of St Barbara**, one of the most beautiful and unusual medieval buildings in Central Europe. At its peak Kutná Hora was bigger than London, its currency accepted all over Europe, its wealth one of the foundations of the power and prestige of the monarchs enthroned in Prague. The good times came to an end

PRAGUE – EXCURSIONS

in the 16th century, when the silver was worked out; the town shrank to a third of its former size and much of it was later burnt down. Far from helping to support Prague, Kutná Hora now needs outside aid to prop up its crumbling heritage.

The triple tent-like roofs of the Church of St Barbara rise from a forest of flying buttresses, spikes and turrets giving it a fantastic outline. Dedicated to the patron saint of miners, sappers and artillerymen, it was begun in 1388 to an over-ambitious design and consequently never completed. Much of its present appearance is due to the carefully considered early 16th-century modifications made to the original plan by Benedikt Ried, architect of the Vladislav Hall in Prague's castle. Just as in Prague, he gave Gothic vaulting

Kutná Hora: a view from the gardens of the Italian Court

a final twist of inventiveness, creating complex patterns of stunning beauty.

There is much else to see in Kutná Hora: the great **Church of St Jakub** with its tall tower, the long façade of the **Jesuit College**, the Hradek, housing the **Mining Museum**, and fine burghers' residences. But the town's second great monument is the **Vlášský dvůr (Italian Court)**, the former mint, which owes its name to the Italian specialists brought in at beginning of the 14th century to turn the silver into coinage. It also served as a royal residence and later as the Town Hall. Much restored in the 19th century, it has a pretty courtyard, a royal chapel, and a museum with examples of the coins minted here.

Trains to Kutná Hora are infrequent, and the town is a good 45-minute walk from the station – so a car is useful for this excursion.

PRACTICALITIES

Accommodation

Centrál, Rybná 8 (tel: 02 232
4351). Basic accommodation in
the Old Town. Disco. Budget.
Club Motel, Průhonice (tel: 02
75 9513). Motorists planning a
brief stop in the Prague area
might consider this well-
equipped motel on the Brno
motorway just outside the city
at leafy Pruhonice. Moderate
to expensive.
Diplomat, Evropská 15 (tel: 02
331 4111). Unexcitingly but
conveniently located on the
run-in from the airport but only
minutes from the centre from
Dejvická Metro, this is a
businessmen's favourite.
Restaurant, nightclub, airport
shuttle etc. Expensive.
Harmony, Napoříčí 31 (tel: 232
00 16). Recently rebuilt, on
busy street within easy
walking distance of centre.
Moderate.
Paříž, U Obecního domu 1 (tel:
02 232 2051). Restored Art
Nouveau splendour next to the
wonderful Art Nouveau Obecní
dům (Municipal House). Café.
Expensive.
For private accommodation try
AVE at the Main Station (Hlavní
Nádraží) (tel: 02 236 25 60).

Restaurants

Myslivna, Jagellonská 21 (tel:
02 27 62 09). Prague's best
game restaurant. Moderate.
U maltézských rytířu,
Prokopská 10 (tel: 02 53 63 57).
Gourmet food in Malá Strana
at reasonable prices.
Moderate.
U tři pštrosů, Dražického
náměstí 6 (tel: 02 53 60 07).
Location (Malá Strana end of

A refreshment break in the city

Charles Bridge) and ambience
(17th-century interiors) couldn't
be bettered. Bohemian and
international. Expensive.
U zlaté hrušky, Novy svět 3
(tel: 02 53 11 33). In the most
picturesque street in Hradčany;
choice of international or
Bohemian specialities.
Expensive.

Cafés

Evropa, Václavské náměstí 25.
The archetypal Central
European café, part of the
famous hotel.
Obecní dům, Náměstí
Republiky. Sumptuous Art
Nouveau setting in the
Municipal House.

Pubs

U fleků, Kremencová 11, New
Town. Medieval courtyard
somehow absorbs the
hundreds of tourists getting
their share of the pub's famous
black beer. Unmissable.
U kocoura, Nerudova 2, Malá
Strana. The 'Tomcat' serves
Pilsner in an authentic setting on
the way up to the castle.

WESTERN BOHEMIA

(See map on pages 24 and 25)

On the map, the westernmost region of the Czech Republic points like an arrowhead at Germany; links with the Germanic world have always been strong here, if not necessarily amiable. The old industrial and brewing city of Plzeň (Pilsen) stands on the ancient highway linking Prague to the great Bavarian cities of Nuremberg and Regensburg, while medieval Domažlice is the miniature capital of the Chods, a mysterious ethnic group once employed by the Bohemian kings to guard the vulnerable frontier. In the far northwest is Cheb, another border town, betraying its Germanic origins with a surfeit of steep-pitched roofs and dormer windows. Here, too, is the cluster of world-famous spa towns, Karlovy Vary (Carlsbad), Mariánské Lázně (Marienbad) and Františkovy Lázně, once serving an aristocratic clientele which was drawn from all over the continent.

The borders with Germany are clearly defined by well forested ranges; along the boundary with Saxony run the Krušné hory (Ore Mountains), dropping sharply to the deep trench through which the Ohře River flows east to join the Labe (Elbe). The once splendid conifer forest of the Ore Mountains has been badly affected by atmospheric pollution generated not just locally but in Germany too; attempts are now being made to replant with more resistant

tree species. The uplands to the southwest are less dramatic, rising gently on either side of the Bohemian/Bavarian border through woodland which has suffered less from acid rain and other environmental ills.

◆◆
CHEB

Once known as the Bohemian Nuremberg because of its wealth of ancient timber-framed houses, the border town of Cheb retains some of its power to charm, in spite of only partially successful attempts to breathe new life into it after the enforced departure of its German inhabitants in 1945. Cheb was originally a Slav stronghold on the banks of the

Red-roofed houses in the beautiful historic centre of Cheb

Ohře River, but was soon Germanised and given the name of Eger. By the 12th century it had become an Imperial city, one of the principal seats of the great Emperor Frederick Barbarossa. Though it later became part of Bohemia, it retained a kind of independence; its people, together with those of the surrounding Egerland, clung fiercely to their traditional ways and remained bitter opponents of any forms of encroachment by the Czechs.

The historic centre of the town is formed by the market square (Náměstí krále Jiřího z Poděbrad). Lined with buildings of various dates, this generously sized civic space is presided over by a stalwart Roland figure atop his fountain. The baroque **Radnice (Town Hall)** houses a gallery of modern Czech art, but more intriguing, beyond the Hercules fountain at the far end of the square, is the extravagantly picturesque group of free-standing medieval buildings known as the **Špaliček**. Behind the Špaliček stands the Renaissance house in which Albrecht von Wallenstein was done to death on 25 February 1634. This great commander of the Emperor's armies in the Thirty Years' War was suspected of Imperial ambitions himself; his assassination was the work of an Englishman, an Irishman and a Scotsman. The building is now the town **Museum**, with excellent local collections and Wallenstein memorabilia.

Cheb has a number of churches, of which Sv Mikuláš (St Nicholas), in a mixture of styles, is the most impressive, but its other main sight consists of the substantial remains of the **Imperial castle**. Among the baroque fortifications on the banks of the river are the ruins of Barbarossa's Great Hall, a two-storey chapel and a sturdy keep built of basalt blocks.

◆◆
DOMAŽLICE

Almost on the border with Bavaria, Domažlice is the westernmost of all Czech towns, the capital of the ethnic group known as the Chods. Its long market square with its arcaded houses makes a fine introduction to the delights of Bohemian townscapes.

In the Middle Ages, the Chods gained privileges as guardians of the frontier of the Bohemian kingdom. Though their special status was later revoked (they supported the wrong side in the Thirty Years' War), they have maintained their distinct identity among the Czechs, most obviously displayed at their annual festival in August, when much jollification takes place to the sound of bagpipes.

Closed at its eastern end by the massive Lower Gate, the market square is a study of variations on the theme of decorative gables, in Renaissance, baroque and Empire styles. The slightly off-kilter church tower can be climbed for a wonderful view of the town. Two museums aim to give visitors an impression of the traditional life of the Chods; one is housed in the round-towered **Chodský hrad (castle)**, the other, the **Jindřich Jindřich Ethnographical Museum**, is based on the collections which were assembled by the locally born composer of that name.

◆◆
FRANTIŠKOVY LÁZNĚ

'Cheb water' had already gained a reputation in the 12th century, but it was only towards the very end of the 18th century that a spa settlement began to be laid out around the two dozen mineral springs set among the woodlands just to the north of Cheb.

Given the name Franzensbad (Francis Spa) in honour of the then Emperor Franz II, Františkovy Lázně is the most tranquil of the three spas making up the 'Bohemian Triangle' which includes Karlovy Vary and Mariánské Lázně. Its mostly classical buildings, many of them still painted in 'Habsburg yellow', stand in fresh green parkland, through which serpentine paths wind their way to various springs. The focal point of the spa is the pavilion housing the **Františkův pramen (Francis Spring)**; near by, holding a fish in rather unsubtle symbolism, is a bronze cherub, much fingered by female patients in superstitious search of a cure for their infertility.

Accommodation

Slovan, Národní 5 (tel: 0166 942 841). Refurbished turn of the century establishment with good restaurant. Moderate.

The Bohemian dollar

The old mining town of Jáchymov lies high up in one of the valleys cut into the Krušné hory (Ore Mountains) by the tributaries of the River Ohře. Silver was discovered here in the early 16th century, miners were brought in from Saxony, and the place was given the German name of St Joachimsthal. A mint was established, and before long the silver coins known as 'Joachimsthaler', or 'Thaler' for short, were common currency. Not many people realise that the 'dollar' was invented in this corner of northwest Bohemia, nor that during its heyday before the Thirty Years' War the town was second only to Prague in importance. In the 19th century it was discovered that a by-product of silver mining was uranium, and in 1900 it was from Joachimsthal uranium that Marie Curie first isolated radium. The warm radioactive springs here were subsequently harnessed to treat various complaints, though this particular 'cure' seems to have been little help to the uranium miners, who even in the 1930s had a life expectancy of not much more than 40. The early post-war Communist regime sent its political prisoners here for forced labour.

◆◆◆
KARLOVY VARY (CARLSBAD) ✓

The founding legend of this most famous of all spa towns describes how its waters came to the notice of Emperor Charles IV when his hunting dogs fell howling into a hot spring in 1348. It seems, however, that their therapeutic properties may have been known even earlier; what is certain is that over the centuries, people have been flocking here, ostensibly to cure their ills by bathing in and later drinking the sulphurous waters flowing at temperatures of

Spa town elegance in the legendary Karlovy Vary (Carlsbad)

WESTERN BOHEMIA

between 104° and 160° F (42° and 73° C) from the many springs. The guest list goes back to the 16th century, but among the kings and emperors, financiers and statesmen, generals and musicians, one visitor stands out; the greatest of German writers, Johann Wolfgang von Goethe, came here no fewer than 13 times. His many musings on the pleasures of spas include lines urging his fellow-guests not to take the cure too seriously, but to let the good times (*das lustige Leben*) roll. Goethe seems to have taken his own advice seriously enough, leaving Mrs Goethe at home, and, at the age of 70 plus, meeting the last of his many loves, the 17-year-old Ulrike von Levetzov, daughter of a hotel-keeper at nearby Mariánské Lázně.

Karlovy Vary's social appeal is enhanced by its site, a deep wooded valley carved by the winding River Teplá on its way to join the broader Ohře at the northern, modern end of town. Hotels, villas, bath-houses and colonnades, much of their architecture the ultimate in 19th century opulence, fill the valley bottom and spread up along the lower slopes wherever the gradient permits. Most of the spa area is traffic-free, permitting relaxed enjoyment of this splendid setting.

The heart of the spa is the majestic colonnade known as the **Mlýnská kolonáda**, a classical structure of great dignity housing no fewer than four springs. This is perhaps the best place to observe conscientious spa guests

imbibing the waters from the regulation little cup with its curious spout.

In complete contrast to the majesty of the Mlýnská kolonáda is the playful turn-of-the-century colonnade in Dvořák Park, a delicate composition in wrought iron. This is passed on the way north to the **Thermal Sanatorium**, a massive complex completed in 1977, and really the only modern intrusion that has been made into Karlovy Vary's otherwise intact spascape.

To the south, in the area around the marketplace, there are architectural reminders of the antiquity of the town: a baroque plague column of 1776, the tower of the castle, dating back to the time of Charles IV, and the wonderful St Mary Magdalen Church, the masterpiece of architect Kilian Ignaz Dietzenhofer. The most vigorous of the spa's springs is the **Vřídlo**, spouting out 440 gallons (2,000 litres) of hot water at the rate of up to 60 times a minute. Further south still, the section of riverside promenade called Stará louka was once (and may well be again) lined with branches of Europe's most fashionable shops, serving particularly the guests staying in the **Grand Hotel Pupp**. This mother of hotels was founded in 1793 and rebuilt in wedding cake style at the end of the 19th century. After a spell as the Moskva, it has now reverted to the name of its first proprietor, pastry-cook Johann Pupp. Far up the slope on the opposite bank of the river, in self-conscious rivalry to

Crowds still come to take the waters – and other refreshments

the Pupp, stands the equally massive **Imperial**; it was completed just before the outbreak of World War I, the event which signalled the end of the aristocratic world which had made Carlsbad its outdoor drawing room. A funicular still hoists guests from the Pupp up to the viewpoint at Diana's Tower; from here a network of paths leads gently through the oaks and beeches to other features like the memorial to Peter the Great.

Indoor attractions were never lacking here. A long-standing musical tradition included the first performance of Dvořák's New World Symphony, and nowadays, as well as the annual Music Festival named after that composer, there is an annual Film Festival. Luxury products were made and sold, including glass and porcelain; examples

can be seen in the **Museum**, while the **Art Gallery** concentrates on 20th-century Czech painting. Twelve of Carlsbad's many springs are tapped; there is a 13th, supposedly even more effective: the herbal liquor which is called Becherovka after its early 19th-century inventor, Dr Becher.

Accommodation

Astoria, Vřídelní 23 (tel: 017 282 24). Right by the Vřídlo, a wonderful Art Nouveau confection with a more sober interior. Moderate.

Grand Hotel Pupp, Mírové Square (tel: 017 221 21). Quite clearly *the* place to stay and eat in town and possibly still just affordable. Expensive.

WESTERN BOHEMIA

◆◆
LOKET

This tiny medieval fortified town has one of the most picturesque sites in the whole of Bohemia – a rock outcrop almost completely surrounded by an 'elbow' (*loket*) in the course of the Ohře River.

Loket's grim **castle** completely dominates the scene. It was built in the 12th century, abandoned as a stronghold after the Thirty Years' War, then served as a prison. It gives a fine view of the town in its sylvan surroundings, but both the castle and its porcelain museum are temporarily closed for refurbishment.

Far below, the town is distinguished by its curving and sloping marketplace, lined with medieval houses and with an exceptionally fine plague column at its centre. The Bílý kůň (White Horse Inn) was a favourite stopping-off place for Goethe on his way to and from his sojourns in Bohemian spas.

◆◆◆
MARIÁNSKÉ LÁZNĚ (MARIENBAD)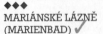

Still better known in the West by its old German name of Marienbad, this is the most recent (though still venerable) of the Bohemian Triangle of spas. Quite distinct from Karlovy Vary, crowded along the river in a deep wooded gorge, or Františkový Lázně, set among its forested flatlands, Mariánské Lázně is laid out in a sumptuously landscaped broad valley floor, its parks and gardens as important to its character as its elegant buildings. More than 900 feet (600m) above sea level, it has a fresher climate than its rivals, and its waters, used to treat a variety of ills, are cold, flowing from some 40 springs at a temperature of between 48° and 52° F (9° and 12° C). Long in the possession of the

Mariánské Lázně

abbots of nearby Teplá, the springs were developed at the beginning of the 19th century, though the first primitive timber bath-house had been erected by the abbey doctor in 1791. The spa was officially opened in 1818 and soon caught on; it was here, in 1820, that Goethe first met his Ulrike. The various springs were capped and set in pavilions of mostly classical design. Mariánské Lázně's heyday was in the late 19th and early 20th centuries, when it was the resort of kings and emperors, the place where Britain's Edward VII wined, dined and dallied, and tried to patch up quarrels with his Germanic cousins between rounds of golf.

The town stretches a long distance north from the nondescript area around the station, its silent trolley buses a useful and pollution-free means of transport. A long and imposing row of balconied edifices facing east across Hlavní třída leads to the head of the valley, where most of the spa installations are housed. Spa guests gather to watch the computer controlled displays of the new Singing Fountain, behind which stretches the town's most stunning single structure, the great cast iron **Colonnade** of 1889, recently restored to its original splendour. Over 390 feet (120m) long, it winds along towards the heart of the spa, the **Křížový (Cross Spring)**, in its delightful little classical pavilion topped by a cross.

The great Goethe is recalled by the square named after him (Goethevo náměstí). Down the slope is the massive drum of the neo-Byzantine Church of the Assumption, while towards the top, among the hotels, is the **Museum**, housed in the building originally called the Golden Grape, where Goethe stayed in 1824.

Accommodation
Grandhotel Praha, Hlavní třída 67 (tel: 0165 59 11). Traditional spa hotel luxury, with excellent restaurant. Expensive.
Kavkaz, Goethovo náměstí 9 (tel: 0165 31 41). A wedding cake edifice, one of Edward VII's favourites. Moderate.

◆◆
PLZEŇ (PILSEN)
This major industrial city sits squarely in the centre of West Bohemia astride the highway from Prague to Nuremberg, famous for its great engineering works and above all for its often imitated but never excelled Pilsner, prototype of all lager beers.

Plzeň originated in the 13th century as a planned town, a replacement for an old Slav fortress a little way up the valley of the Úslava, and the city centre has kept its strict chequerboard layout through a long and sometimes turbulent history (which included Allied bombing attacks in World War II). Industrialisation began in the early 19th century, and by the 1860s Emil Škoda's engineering products were beginning to make his name famous (the car that now carries his name is manufactured at Mladá Boleslav in East Bohemia). His factories were a mainstay of the Austro-Hungarian war effort in 1914-18, and were turned to the same purpose under the Nazi Protectorate (hence the bombing). Pilsner beer rose to prominence in the 19th century too, though its origins go back much further, to when the citizens had the right to brew and sell their own beer, provided it met exacting quality standards. During the 1840s, the individual brewers combined to found a modern brewery; the local water proved to be ideal in the brewing of a bottom-fermented beer, and within a few years Pilsner was being exported all over Europe.

The grand centre of the city is **Náměstí Republiky (Republic Square)**, large enough to act as a fit setting for the equally grand free-standing Gothic Church, whose north steeple, 338 feet (103m) high, is the tallest in the country. In the church's Šternberk Chapel is a lovely late Gothic Madonna. Though much of the centre has been rebuilt, the square retains the feeling of being the focal point of an important historic city, with a number of fine old buildings, of which the most prominent is the Renaissance **Radnice (City Hall)**. The sgraffito work which can be seen on its façade (and elsewhere in the city) was actually added in the early 20th century, but is entirely in the spirit of the original.

The parkland and gardens which have replaced the defensive walls and moats of the old town make an attractive setting for the **Západočeské múzeum (West Bohemian Museum)**, with extensive local collections and good 20th-century painting, as well as for the **Divadlo J K Tyla (Tyl Theatre)**; Tyl was a prolific 19th-century dramatist, some of whose lines were selected in 1918 to be used as lyrics for the national anthem.

Most visitors will want to visit the main brewery. The pedestrian way there runs eastward from the square along Prazska to the medieval **Masné krámy (Butchers' Stalls)** and the 16th-century water tower, part of the city fortifications. A short diversion north can be made to the **Pivovarské muzeum (Museum of Brewing)**, housed in a medieval malthouse. Beyond the River Radbuza, the **Západočeské pivovary (West Bohemian Brewery)** announces itself with a triumphal arch. The guided tour of the brewery is an experience which should not be missed. Even those who are not particularly fond of beer will be impressed by the 5 miles (9km) of cellars and by the exuberant decoration of establishment's own beer hall.

Accommodation

Central, Náměstí Republiky 33 (tel: 019 226 059). As its name suggests, this triumph of 1960s modernism stands right on the main square. Expensive.
Slovan, Smetanovy sady 1 (tel: 019 335 51). Just outside the centre and rather run down, but full of turn-of-the-century character. Moderate.

SOUTH BOHEMIA

(*See map on page 24 and 25*)

From the gentle forest slopes of the Šumava uplands, where the Vltava rises to the pond-studded landscape around Třeboň, much of southern Bohemia has a tranquil, harmonious quality, with few large towns or major industries disturbing its essentially rural character. Present calm appearances can sometimes conceal an eventful history; in the 15th century the hilltop town of Tábor was the great stronghold of the Hussites, from which they defied Church and Crown, initiating a radical and dissenting tradition which could not be further from the near-feudal social conditions which prevailed over much of the south of the area until within

Hussite leader Jan Žižka summons the troops in Tábor's museum

living memory. All around are castles and country seats – like Krumlov, Třeboň, Jindřichův Hradec, Hluboká – from which great families, such as the Vitkoveks, the Rozmberks and the Schwarzenbergs, held sway. The region's location, astride trade routes connecting Prague with the Germanic lands to the south, produced great wealth, which paid for fine buildings in the squares and streets of places like Prachatice or České Budějovice, south Bohemia's capital. The legacy of historic towns is a wonderful counterpoint to the pleasures of walking on 'Europe's Green Roof', the unspoiled woodland rolling uninterruptedly to the Bavarian border.

Detail from the Samson Fountain

◆◆◆
ČESKÉ BUDĚJOVICE ✓

Capital of southern Bohemia, České Budějovice is a sizeable place, its splendid historic core embedded in industrial suburbs, the home of famous products (Kohinoor pencils) and a beer (Budvar/Budweiser) second only to Pilsner in reputation.

All roads lead to Budejovice's splendid main square, **Náměstí Přemysla Otakara II**, without doubt one of the finest urban spaces in Europe. Together with the rest of the Old Town, it was laid out in the 13th century by King Ottokar II of Bohemia in order to assert authority in the southern part of his realm, and

give a signal to the powerful local lords, the Vitkovek clan, not to get too big for their boots. At the confluence of the Vltava and Malše, the low-lying site was drained and defended by walls and towers with additional protection provided by moats formed by arms of the rivers. On the route between the salt mines of Austria and Prague, the place soon prospered, becoming the kingdom's third city (after Prague and Plzeň). Most of its burghers were German-speakers, but in the 19th century the growth of industry drew in Czech workers from the countryside, and the town eventually took on an almost wholly Czech character. The importance of the old salt route was confirmed when the continent's first horse-drawn railway was built between here and Linz on the Danube in 1827. The square's sides, 436 feet (133m) long, are lined with arcaded burghers' houses, many of them medieval, though all have later Renaissance, baroque or classical façades. The most prominent building is the Radnice (Town Hall), a fanciful baroque structure with triple towers and fierce-looking metal gargoyles. A splendidly appropriate central ornament is provided by the Samson Fountain of 1727, but the dominant feature is just off-stage: the **Černá věž (Black Tower)**, rising above the houses at the square's northeastern corner. A fine structure erected in 1577, it houses the bells of the adjacent and much restored baroque **cathedral**, and is 236 feet (72m) to the tip of its flattened onion dome. A trifling 360 steps lead up to the viewing gallery, from where there is a terrific panorama over the town and the surrounding countryside rising gently to the wooded hills which mark the frontier with Austria to the south.

The street pattern still conforms to the plan laid out by the Royal Surveyor in 1265; there are countless fine old houses, perhaps the best being the sgraffitoed **Kneislův dům (Kneisl House)**, beyond the cathedral in Kanovnická Street. Near by, the 17th-century Church of St Anne is now a college. The most interesting buildings are to the west, like the 16th-century **Masné krámy (Butchers' Stalls)**, the **Dominikánský klášter (Dominican Monastery)**, and the **Solnice (Salt Store)**, dating from 1531, with crow's-step gables and three enigmatic carved faces staring from its façade. There are remains of the town fortifications; to the north is the **Rabenstejnská věž (Rabenstein Tower)**, to the south a bastion incorporating the **Železná panná (Iron Maiden Tower)**.

Accommodation, food and drink

Masné krámy, Krajinská 23. Worth a butcher's at the butcher's for beer and food. Closes at 21.00hrs.

Zvon, Náměstí Přemysla Otakara II 28 (tel: 038 353 61). The old 'Bell' Hotel has plenty of atmosphere. The ground floor restaurant is cheaper than the upstairs eatery.

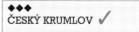

♦♦♦ ČESKÝ KRUMLOV ✓

In 1947 this exquisite medieval town and its great castle suffered an almost terminal shock when their aristocratic rulers were dispossessed after a reign that had begun with the site's foundation in the 13th century. Combined with the loss of its largely German population, indifference and insufficient funds for conservation, Krumlov slowly mouldered away. But key buildings and interiors were preserved, and it seems likely that UNESCO designation will prove the turning point in the salvation of the town.

Overlooked by the castle on its rock, the core of the town is crammed on to a lesser height, almost totally enclosed by a loop in the Vltava. It was laid out in the middle of the 13th century by the local lords, the Vitkovek clan, at the foot of the fortress they had founded to command the important north-south trade route along the river. The Vitkoveks were succeeded by the Rožmberks, who remodelled and extended the castle in an attempt to turn it into a Renaissance palace. They in turn gave way to the Schwarzenbergs, who ruled here until 1947; until nearly the end, they maintained their private army of a dozen gaudily uniformed retainers, and a trumpeter sounded the hours from the castle's high tower. The **castle** (you must buy a ticket and join a tour) is the biggest in the country after Prague's Hradčany, extending

SOUTH BOHEMIA

westwards along a narrow ridge between the Vltava and a minor stream to the north, in the process jumping a deep ravine by means of an extraordinary multi-tiered bridge. The complex, almost city-like structure has several courtyards and some 300 rooms. Bears pad around the moat and cannon adorn one of the courtyards. The base of the tower formed part of the original 13th century stronghold; its elaborate cap with viewing gallery is one of the most splendid creations of its kind in the country, added in the late 16th century. Interminable interiors include some marvellous things, among them the **Maškarní sál (Ballroom)**, decorated in the mid-18th century with *trompe-l'oeil* paintings featuring the capering characters of the Italian *commedia dell'arte*. The bridge leads to the extensive grounds of the castle, but first to the **theatre**. This is one of the most complete 18th-century theatres in existence, forming the perfect setting for a courtly performance of a minor opera. Today's performances take place in a later, outdoor theatre, built in the castle park in the 1950s.

Krumlov town seduces by its overall charm rather than by the outstanding quality of particular buildings. Its roofscapes are particularly fine, while the streets, as they dip and twist, form a succession of continuously changing and intricate views. Široká ulice (Broad Street) has some of the grander houses. The focal point is the main square, **Náměstí svornosti**, with the arcaded Renaissance Radnice (Town Hall) and a plague column. Horní ulice (Upper Street) climbs eastwards, to the early 16th-century **Kaplánka House** with its oriel window; behind it

Český Krumlov seen from the massive castle walls

is the town's other dominant feature, the splendid steep-roofed and tall-towered Gothic **St Vitus' Church**, perched above the river. Close to the bridge, which spans the defensive ditch cut through a narrow isthmus formed by the Vltava, is the the 16th-century building of the Hotel Růže, once a college of the Jesuits. In their old Seminary opposite is the local **Museum**.

From the square there is a narrow descent to the bridge over the Vltava, then a curving rise past the little **St Justus Church**, whose tower, in combination with the castle, features in so many photographs of the town. Steps lead up to the outer courtyard of the castle and the old Town Hall of the Latrán quarter. Down by the bending river is a convent (now an old people's home) and the old arsenal (now a brewery). Guarding the entrance to the Latran is the imposing Budějovice Gate, an Italian design dating from the late 16th century.

Accommodation

Krumlov, Náměstí svornosti 14 (tel: 0337 22 55). Old establishment on the main square. Restaurant. Moderate. **Růže**, Horní ulice 153 (tel: 0337 22 45). Even more atmospheric than the Krumlov and equally well located. Moderate. **Vyšehrad**, (tel: 0337 23 51). Krumlov is a district centre, and its outskirts feature a number of modern blocks like this hotel, which fortunately do not intrude into the old townscape. Restaurant. Budget.

Ballroom capers in Český Krumlov

◆◆◆
HLUBOKÁ

Often compared with England's Windsor Castle, mock-Tudor Hluboká is the country's most visited castle after the Hrad in Prague.

A royal stronghold had been erected on the rock commanding the Vltava by Ottokar II, as part of his strategy to keep the ambitious Vitkoveks in check. After many alterations and changes of ownership, the castle came in to the possession of the Schwarzenbergs in 1670. Baroquified in the following century, it was completely rebuilt in the middle of the 19th century according to the owners' idiosyncratic vision of late-medieval England. This conjuring up of a past that never existed did not exclude amenities like central heating, and the wood-burning system which was installed in the 1860s is still functioning.

The castle has over 140 rooms, many of them lavishly furnished with what the Schwarzenbergs left behind on their departure at the end of World War II, supplemented by other objects installed here by their successor, the State. Among the portraits, glass, porcelain and weapons are a number of outstanding tapestries. Entered via the elaborate iron and glass Winter Garden, the Riding School now serves as the **South Bohemian Art Gallery**, its star exhibits the charming Madonnas on whom the late Gothic painters of the South Bohemian School lavished much love.

By the banks of the great fishpond southwest of the castle is the Schwarzenbergs' **Hunting Lodge** (Ohrada), housing a museum of huntin', shootin' and fishin' (and loggin').

PRACHATICE

Backed by the green hills of the Šumava rising to the southwest, pretty Prachatice is one of the most perfectly preserved and attractive historic towns of southern Bohemia, with the buildings of its old core still tightly packed behind the oval of medieval walls.

Prachatice's importance came from its position on the Golden Way; it was from here that Austrian salt from the mines around Salzburg was

distributed all over Bohemia. In Renaissance times the town blossomed under the overlordship of the Rožmberk family, and it was during this period that much of the sgraffito decoration of its old buildings was carried out, best seen on **Velké náměstí (Main Square)**. The elaborate patterning on the façade of the **Stará radnice (Old Town Hall)** is particularly striking, some of its lively scenes based on works by Holbein. Just off the square is the steep-roofed and tall-towered late Gothic Church of Sv Jakub, a landmark from far around, and behind it the splendid **Písek Gate**, the most impressive part of the fortifications.

Every evening at 10 o'clock the bell is still rung which once served to indicate Prachatice's whereabouts to pack-horse drivers who might have strayed from the Golden Way.

Accommodation

Zlatá stezka, Velké náměstí (tel: 0338 218 41). The 'Golden Way' is right on the main square. Restaurant. Moderate.

ŠUMAVA MOUNTAINS

These uplands rise gently from the interior of Bohemia to form a wooded border with Bavaria and the northwestern tip of Austria. The scenery is tranquil rather than dramatic; the summits tend to be rounded, and there are dark lakes and ancient woodland. Upland pastures interrupt the otherwise

Prachatice market

SOUTH BOHEMIA

The gentle Šumava uplands

continuous cover of beech, spruce and fir; there is little arable land and settlements are few and far between. Rainfall is abundant, feeding peat bogs and the rivers which have their source here, among them the Teplá ('warm') and Studená ('cold') branches of the Vltava. It's ideal walking country, especially since the demolition of the Iron Curtain, whose unsightly installations were at their most impregnable along an ultra-sensitive frontier. There's winter activity, too, at the modest ski resorts of Železná Ruda and Churanov. Semi-feudal conditions persisted in the Šumava (in German Böhmerwald, or Bohemian Forest) until very recent times, the sparse population of herdsmen, woodmen and glass-makers remaining closely tied to the great landowners like the Schwarzenbergs. Not that the latter were averse to progress; in the late 18th century they built an extraordinary engineering work, a 32-mile (52km) flume for floating timber down to the Danube, and in the 19th century they designated Europe's first nature reserve, part of the Boubín primeval forest. Conservation continues today; the greater part of the Šumava is a National Park, with strong links across the border to the **Nationalpark Bayrischer Wald (Bavarian Forest National Park)**.

The Šumava can be approached from a number of centres. Domažlice and Klatovy form its northern gateways, while further to the southeast is the old town of **Sušice**, famous for its match factory and with the **Šumava Museum** housed in the town's most striking building, the Gothic-cum-

Renaissance Veprchovský dům
on the main square.
Overlooked by castle ruins,
Kašperské Hory is an old gold-
mining town with a branch of
the Šumava Museum
specialising in glassware. Little
Vimperk, on the Prague-
Passau highway, also has a
museum, laid out in some of the
rooms of the Schwarzenberg
castle overlooking the town.
Vimperk is the starting point for
walks around the edge of the
strictly protected **Boubínský
prales**, the primeval forest
cladding the slopes of Boubín
(3,264 feet/1,362m). A winding
railway line climbs up to the
country's highest station at
Kubova Hut (995 metres).
Volary is famous for its timber-
built houses of Alpine type; to
the south near **Jeleni** is one of
the tunnels of the
Schwarzenberg flume, as well
as a memorial to the last
Bohemian bear, done to death
here in 1856.
Probably the most popular of
the Šumava's attractions is the
immensely long **Lipno Lake**,
created in the 1950s to generate
hydroelectric power from the
Vltava. In summer its surface is
alive with dinghies, rowboats
and canoes, its shoreline
crowded with chalets and
campers. The railway and a trio
of roads connect the lake with
Český Krumlov. The village of
Horní Plana (Oberplan), on the
north bank, was the birthplace
of the 19th-century Austrian
writer, Adalbert Stifter; little
read nowadays, his novels and
short stories portray the
landscapes of the
Šumava/Böhmerwald with deep

affection. One of his favourite
spots was the **Plesné jezero
(Plockensteinsee)**, the
romantic lake beneath the
summit of the highest point in
the Šumava, Plechy, 4,521 feet
(1,378m) high and accessible
only on foot.

TÁBOR
Named after the mountain top in
the Holy Land where Christ's
transfiguration took place, this
old town crowning a hilltop, 56
miles (90km) south of Prague, is
the place most closely
identified with the turbulent
followers of Jan Hus.
Led by the one-eyed military
genius Jan Žižka, the Hussites
set up their encampment here
(*tábor* means 'camp' in Czech)
in 1420 after having fled
Prague, quickly making it into a
stronghold for their religious
and social beliefs, and from
which they issued, sword in
hand, to propagate them in
Bohemia and beyond.
The chaotic layout of the town,
designed to confuse intruders,
dates from Hussite times, and
it's still a confusing experience
to wander around the maze of
shabby alleyways. Eventually,
however, you are bound to
emerge in **Žižkovo náměstí
(Žižkov Square)**, lined with
burghers' houses whose
façades are of Renaissance or
later date (though a medieval
structure may lurk behind the
gables). Below the surface runs
a labyrinth of tunnels and
cellars, reached from the **Stará
radnice (Old Town Hall)**,
which now houses the Museum,
with its excellent displays on

the Hussite movement. The highly picturesque three-gabled façade of the Town Hall is a 19th-century interpretation of what Renaissance architects should have done, but the Council Chamber dates from 1515 and has a coat of arms incorporating statuettes of Hus and Žižka. Completed at about the same time, the Church of the Transfiguration in the northwest corner of the square has even more splendid vaulting as well as a 252-foot (77m) tower.

From the square, Pražská ulice (Prague Street) runs east towards modern Tábor, while to the west Klokotská ulice is closed by the massive **Bechyně Gate**, with its extravagantly steep-pitched roof, next to the round tower of the town's castle.

Accommodation, food and drink

Beseda, Žižkovo náměstí. Old-style restaurant set right on the main square.

Palcat, Třída 9 května (tel: 0361 22 901). Anonymous 1960s box, just outside the old town with good views from some rooms. Restaurant. Moderate.

◆◆
TŘEBOŇ

Much of the wealth of the lords of this tiny town came from the chain of great fishponds laid out from medieval times onwards in the marshy lowlands along the course of the River Lužnice. A mere 656 feet by 1,312 feet (200m by 400m) within its walls, Trebon is only a fraction of the size of the pond on whose banks it stands, the **Svět (World Pond)** of 1571. The town's

southwest corner is filled with the **castle**, owned by the Rožmberks and the Schwarzenbergs in succession; its last Rožmberk proprietor was Petr Vok, *bon viveur* and dabbler in alchemy, who died from the effects of good living in 1611. It has a series of fine courtyards and furnished rooms, and houses an important historical archive as well as an informative **Fisheries Museum**. The pretty main square, little more than an expanded street, has a fountain and plague column and is lined with attractive 16th to 18th-century houses; the Town Hall of 1566 faces the slightly earlier Bílý koníček (White Horse Inn). The southern entrance to the town is guarded by two gates, between them the historic **Třeboň Brewery**, whose origins go back to the 14th century.

There are some 6,000 ponds in this part of southern Bohemia, some linked by a long canal, the **Zlatá stoka (Golden Canal)**, dug in the 16th century. To the north of Třebon is the biggest pond of all, the 3 square-mile (7 sq km) inland sea, formed at the same time as the canal and named after the Rožmberks, the **Rožmberský rybník**.

Accommodation

Bílý koníček, Hlavní náměstí (tel: 0333 22 48). Unbeatable central location in one of Třeboň's oldest buildings. Restaurant. Budget.

Svět, Hliník 750–2 (tel: 0333 31 47). Overlooking the Svět pond, this modern hotel is well placed to serve carp and the like in its fish restaurant. Moderate.

NORTH AND EAST BOHEMIA

(*See map on pages 24 and 25*)

Apart from the fertile lowlands along the course of the River Labe (Elbe), much of northern and eastern Bohemia consists of forested uplands, among them the country's highest and most visited mountains, the **Krkonoše (Giant Mountains)**. The highlands' prosperity has always depended not so much on agriculture as on industry of one kind or another. German miners and craftsmen settled here in the Middle Ages, and in Austro-Hungarian times the area formed the industrial heartland of the Habsburg Empire. This is where the intricacies of Bohemian jewellery and glass-making were perfected, followed by the growth of heavy industries based on coal and chemicals. Under Communism, industrial expansion was accelerated; whole towns like Most were moved to make way for draglines digging out the brown coal to feed the power stations which provide much of the country's electricity. In places, atmospheric pollution has reached intolerable levels. High altitude woodland has suffered the worst damage, leaving intact the fine forest setting of the **České středohoří (Central Bohemian Heights)** and of the extraordinary rock formations called (not altogether inappropriately) the **Český ráj (Bohemian Paradise)** and **České Švýcarsko (Bohemian Switzerland)**.

◆◆
ČESKÝ RÁJ (BOHEMIAN PARADISE)

Ever since their discovery by poets and painters in the early 19th century, these fantastic rock formations rising from the pinewoods have exerted a pull on people's imagination. Less than an hour from Prague by motorway, they are one of the

Dramatic beauty at Český Ráj

NORTH AND EAST BOHEMIA

country's most popular excursion spots.

To the south of the dull town of Turnov, the sandstones of the Bohemian plateau have weathered to form a whole array of strange features: pinnacles, columns, battlements, blocky masses separated by deep clefts, and the famous 'rock cities' of **Hrubá skála** and **Prachovské skály**, a challenge for climbers perfecting their technique. The area forms an ultra-romantic setting for a number of castles. The ruins of **Valdštejn** were once the ancestral home of the Wallenstein family, whose most famous scion, Albrecht, Imperial Commander in the Thirty Years' War, fell to the assassins' daggers in an upstairs room in Cheb. The twin towers of another ruin, **Trosky**, perch on a brace of basalt crags. Medieval **Kost** is still intact, having survived the indignity of being used as a grain store for many years. It now houses fine late Gothic paintings from the national collection in Prague.

◆
DĚČÍN

Together with its sister town Podmokly, on the left bank of the Labe, Děčín is an important river port, its castle rock the traditional gateway to Bohemia for travellers from Saxony. For today's tourists, however, its significance lies more in its central location among the scenic delights of **České Švýcarsko (Bohemian Switzerland)**, the sandstone uplands through which the river

has cut a deep cleft on its way down to Germany and which have been eroded into fantastic forms. The landscape of rock pinnacles rising dramatically through the forest continues into Germany, where it has inevitably won the name of Saxon Switzerland; one of the best starting points for exploration on the Czech side is the riverside settlement of **Hřensko**, just short of the frontier and easily reached by the steamers which ply up and down the Labe between Decín and Dresden. To the east of the village are walks to features like the natural bridge, **Pravčická brana**, the largest of its kind outside America, or, with the aid of small boats, along the

Hradec Králové

trackless gorges of the River Kamenice.

Accommodation
Labe, (tel: 0412 981 88). As its name implies, nicely situated on the Labe in the popular tourist village of Hřensko. Budget.

◆◆
HRADEC KRÁLOVÉ
Under its German name of Königgrätz, Hradec Králové is famous for the 1866 battle which ended in a spectacular Prussian victory over the Habsburg armies in 1866, but the town is a fascinating place in its own right. Its historic centre on the left bank of the Labe is complemented by the New

Town on the right bank, a masterpiece of urban planning from the days of the First Czechoslovak Republic. With most of its functions transferred to the New Town, the Old Town is a quiet place, its elongated main square (Žižkovo náměstí) forming as fine an urban ensemble as any in Bohemia. The brick cathedral is medieval, the Old Town Hall Renaissance, the Church of St Mary and Bishop's Palace baroque. The **Art Gallery** of 20th-century Czech art is perhaps the best place in the country to make the acquaintance of many relatively unknown modern masters as well as the big names like Mucha. On the banks of the

Labe is the Krajské muzeum
(District Museum), designed by
Kotěra and housing extensive
collections of 19th- and 20th-
century arts and crafts.
Königgrätz has been described
as the 'first battle of modern
warfare', with a quarter of a
million troops assembled on
each side and breech-loading
artillery used to deadly effect
by the Prussians. You might
catch a faint echo of the din of
battle around the village of
Chlum, 6 miles (10km)
northwest of Hradec Králové,
where there are cemeteries and
a viewing tower.

Accommodation
Černigov, Riegrovo náměstí
1499 (tel: 049 340 11). A 1960s
high-rise block, close but not
too close to the main railway
station and one of the town's
main social centres, with two
restaurants, casino, disco etc.
Moderate.

◆◆◆
KRKONOŠE (GIANT MOUNTAINS)
The highest of the ranges
defining the frontiers of
Bohemia, the Giant Mountains
have been protected as a
National Park since 1963. This
has not saved them from the
dire effects of atmospheric
pollution; the forests here have
suffered from acid rain, and
many of the higher areas have a
desolate look, disguised in
winter by the abundant snowfall.
The mountains' popularity
remains undiminished,
however; crowds continue to
arrive from Prague to hike
along the 600 miles (1,000km)

Glass-making is a speciality in the
Krkonoše town of Harrachov

KRKONOŠE

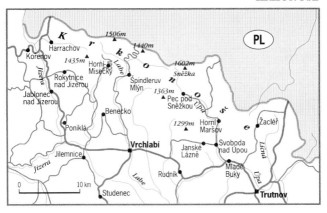

of well-marked footpaths in summer and to practise downhill and cross-country skiing in winter. The area's accessiblity is enhanced by chair lifts, though the proposal to run a cable car up to the highest point, Sněžka, has not been implemented.

The main ridge runs eastwards from above the small glass-making town of **Harrachov**, forming the frontier with Poland. To the south, the Labe and its tributaries flow down glaciated valleys. The mountain tops have always been bare, with a climate rivalling that of much higher ranges for severity and capriciousness; walkers should be well prepared. The forest still flourishes in the attractive valleys, where there are a number of resorts, some of them established for more than a century. **Špindlerův Mlýn** is perhaps the best known, but there are facilities at Harrachov, Rokytnice, Horní Misecky,

Benecko, at the old spa of Janské Lázně and at Pec pod Snežkou. Among the most popular walks are hikes from Špindlerův Mlýn along the infant Labe, past waterfalls to its source in high moorland, or up to **Sněžka** itself (accessible by chairlift, too). Here, the flattened rock-strewn summit is adorned with a number of structures including a chapel dating from 1681. It's also patrolled by border guards. The view must be one of the most sensational in Europe, stretching far over Silesia to the north and sometimes as far as the outskirts of Prague to the southwest.

The 'gateway to the Krkonoše' is the town of **Vrchlabí**, strung out along the river where it crosses the main road which forms the only east-west route along the base of the mountains. As well as a number of baroque buildings and arcaded timber houses the town has the offices of the National Park and an interesting museum of the region.

Accommodation
The best bet in the mountain resorts, whose hotels are often fully booked, is to find a private room, possibly through Cedok in Vrchlabí. Accommodation is traditionally provided in the form of mountain refuges, called *bouda*. Some of these, like the **Labská bouda** (tel: 0438 932 21), high up near the source of the Labe, are far from primitive.
In Špindlerův Mlýn:
Montana, (tel: 0438 935 51). Modern (1970s), good views. Restaurant. Expensive.
Savoy, (tel: 0438 935 21). Turn-of-the-century, self-consciously Alpine hotel. Restaurant. Moderate.

LITOMĚŘICE
On the banks of the Labe, among hop gardens and vineyards, this rather run-down place was one of the earliest towns in Bohemia, the medieval market held in its huge square one of the most important in Europe. Mistakenly choosing the Protestant side in the Thirty Years' War, Litoměřice was vigorously re-Catholicised afterwards, the reason for its abundance of baroque churches, among them the richly furnished **cathedral** and the delightful little **Chapel of Sv Václav (St Wenceslas)**. The **market square** has fine Renaissance and baroque town houses as well as a splendid **Radnice (Town Hall)** and the **Mrazovský dům (Chalice**

House), with its roof in the form of a communion cup. The **Severočeská galérie (Central Bohemian Gallery)** has exceptionally good examples of Czech painting.

LITOMYŠL
This is one of the most exquisite small towns in Bohemia, its irregular, long main square lined with arcaded and gabled burghers' houses. The building known as **U rytířů** stands out, with a particularly jolly decorative scheme. Litomyšl's **castle** is a Renaissance structure of great splendour, with sgraffitoed stonework on the outside, a great arcaded courtyard within, and a completely intact 18th-century theatre. The castle brewery dates from Renaissance times too, but is more famous as the birthplace of the composer Bedřich Smetana, an excellent excuse for the town's annual music festival.

Accommodation
Zlatá hvězda, (tel: 0464 23 38). Central. Budget.

PARDUBICE
This substantial city on the Labe is famous for its steeplechase (the toughest course outside England), and notorious for the explosive Semtex, the prize product of the local chemical industry. Like Hradec Králové, Pardubice has an extensive New Town laid out in the optimistic days of the First Republic; the attractive Old Town was laid out in the 16th

century by the powerful Pernštejn family, then rebuilt after being burnt down by the Swedes in 1645. Linking old and new is Náměstí Republiky (Republic Square), with the Gothic-cum-Renaissance Church of Sv Bartoloměj (St Bartholomew) to the north, the Art Nouveau City Theatre to the south. Beyond the spiked and helmeted 16th-century gateway is **Pernštejnské náměstí (Pernštejn Square)**, with richly decorated Renaissance houses and a late 19th-century Town Hall. Sumptuous decoration characterises the **castle**, the Pernštejn's Renaissance replacement of their original Gothic stronghold (currently under reconstruction).

Accommodation
Interhotel Labe, Masarykovo náměstí 2633 (tel: 040 596 874). **Zlatá stika**, Strossova 127 (tel: 040 518 111). Budget.

◆◆
TEREZÍN
Together with Lidice, Terezín stands as a monument to the brutality of Nazi rule in the Protectorate of Bohemia-Moravia. The grim fortress town was built between 1780 and 790 to block Prussia's way southward into Austria, and given the name Theresienstadt in memory of Empress Maria Theresa. The **Malá pevnost (Little Fortress)** beyond served as a prison, its most famous inmate the Serb Gavrilo Princip, assassin of Archduke Franz Ferdinand at Sarajevo in 1914. It continued in use as a gaol under the Nazis, while the town

Burghers' house, Litomyšl

was made into a ghetto and its inhabitants replaced by the Jewish population of Bohemia-Moravia. Terezín became a kind of perverted showcase for the Final Solution, a place to which the International Red Cross could be invited to show how well Germany was treating her second-class citizens; some kind of normal existence was allowed to continue, but it was all a sham; thousands of people died here, and tens of thousands more were transported to the death camps. The story of Terezin/Theresienstadt is told in moving detail in the Little Fortress and in the new Ghetto Museum in the town itself.

MORAVIA

(*See map on pages 24 and 25*)

Defined by a horseshoe of uplands running from the Czech-Moravian Highlands in the west via the Jeseníky and Beskids to the White Carpathians in the east, the second province of the Czech Lands focuses on its go-ahead capital, Brno, the ancient bishops' city of Olomouc, and the great industrial conurbation around Ostrava. In the lowlands, along the rivers flowing south towards the Danube, fruit and vines benefit from fertile soils and a mild climate. The province has some of the country's key attractions, including the castles of Pernštejn and Vranov and gems of towns like Telč and Kroměříž. Folk traditions persist in the southeast, while the planned town of Zlín makes an intriguing contrast to medieval cityscapes.

Zelný trh – Brno's vegetable market

BRNO ✓

The country's second city and the capital of Moravia, Brno is an ancient place which has moved with the times to become an important commercial and industrial centre. The Industrial Revolution reached here as early as the end of the 18th century, and busy textile mills soon caused the place to be known as *Rakouský Mančestr* (Austrian Manchester). All this activity drew in workers from the Czech countryside, and Brno slowly lost its Germanic character, though German Jewish families dominated much of industrial life until forced to flee the Nazi take-over in 1939. During the previous two decades, Brno established itself as one of the main centres of modern architecture and design in Europe; the **Výstaviště (Exhibition Grounds)** were laid out in 1928 to celebrate the 10th

anniversary of the establishment of Czechoslovakia and became a museum of progressive architecture, still fascinating today. Among the innovatory architects who worked in the city was Mies van der Rohe, who used glass, steel and concrete to built the cool and elegant **Tugendhat House** of 1930. After World War II the remaining German population was forced to head for the Austrian border on foot – the infamous 'Death March of Brno'. Brno is surrounded by extensive and generally unappealing suburbs, but within the belt of ring roads and parkland where the ramparts once stood is the city's compact Old Town. Here history and the present day meet and mix in frequently exciting juxtaposition. With several institutions of higher learning, theatres, concert halls, museums and galleries, Brno is a lively city and a genuine provincial capital.

◆◆◆

A WALK AROUND BRNO

The Old Town is mostly pedestrianised and can only be explored on foot. Begin the walk among the busy morning market stalls of **Zelný trh (vegetable market)**. Centred on the billowing stonework of the baroque Parnassus Fountain, the square slopes up towards the Dietrichstein Palace, now the home of many of the collections of the **Moravské muzeum (Moravian Museum)**. To the southeast, in the **Kostel Nalazerú Sv Kríze**

(Capuchin Church Crypt) is the most macabre sight in the city: a system of vents has kept the kippered corpses of monks and monastic benefactors in a gruesome state of air-dried mummification. To the southwest, **Petersberg (Petrov Hill)** is crowned by the spires and spikes of Brno's cathedral, **Dóm na Petrove**. This basically Gothic building was battered and burnt by the Swedes in the 17th century, baroquified in the 18th, then re-Gothicized in the 19th. Its wonderful silhouette makes it one of the city's landmarks, together with the **Špilberk fortress** topping the rise to the west. To the south, the terraced **Denisové sady (Denis Gardens)** have an obelisk commemorating the end of the Napoleonic Wars, reminding us that Bonaparte stayed in Brno before going on to trounce his opponents at Slavkov (Austerlitz) across the plain to the east.

Biskupská and Dominikánská Streets wind down from the cathedral to the baroque statues guarding the front of **Dominikánský Chrám Sv Michala (Dominican Church)**. Beyond is the **Nová radnice (New City Hall)**, new only in the sense that most of it was built later than the **Stará radnice (Old City Hall)**, whose rear entrance faces Mecová (Sword Street). Inside, there are galleries, offices and the municipal tourist bureau, as well as a couple more oddities, the **Brnenský drak (Brno Dragon)** and the **Brnenské kolo (Brno Wheel)**. The former is no dragon but a crocodile,

MORAVIA – BRNO

foisted on the city by King Matthias in 1608 when he couldn't think what to do with this unwanted Christmas present from the Turks. The wheel was the object of a bet, made from scratch, then rolled here from Lednice, 25 miles (40km) away, all in the course of a day. The Old City Hall has a tall tower which is worth climbing for the view, and its main entrance is graced with an amazingly elongated Gothic portal whose master-mason left the central pinnacle drooping after being cheated out of his full fee by the burghers.

One block to the east, busy Masaryková Street runs into the epicentre of city life, **Náměstí svobody (Liberty Square)**, an irregularly shaped and sloping space with a plague column at the far end. The square is lined with imposing buildings of mostly 19th-century appearance. An exception is No 17, a fine Renaissance town house boldly sgraffitoed in the 1930s. Shoppers and students crowd bustling Česká Street, where the plain façade of the **Avion Hotel** usually stands unnoticed. Built in glass and steel by local architect Bohuslav Fuchs in 1928, it is one of the many functionalist structures which gave Brno a world reputation for modern architecture in the interwar period. Jakubské Street leads eastward into the small square completely dominated by the

BRNO

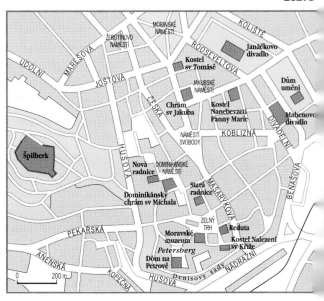

soaring Gothic walls of the **Chrám Sv Jakuba (St James Church),** whose lofty interior has elaborate vaulting and many fine furnishings. A diminutive figure high up above a window unashamedly points his posterior at the public far below; only recently was it discovered that his trouserless state is for the benefit of a hitherto invisible female companion.

At the foot of the gentle slope to the east, where the city walls once stood, are a number of cultural institutions like the **Janáčkovo divadlo (Janáček Theatre)** – Janáček was a Moravian who spent most of his life in Brno, and has a little museum at Smetanová Street 14; the **Mahenovo divadlo (Mahen Theatre)** of 1882 (one of the first of its kind to be lit by electricity, with wiring installed by Edison himself), and the **House of Art**. The Centrum department store, another example of interwar Modernism, was commissioned by Tomas Bata in the late 1920s, and was originally intended to rise 23 storeys high.

On its cramped site at the junction of Jánská Street and Minoritská Street stands the **Minorite Church of St John**, the city's most splendid baroque building, with sumptuous interiors including a Loreto chapel. You can end the walk by returning uphill to the Zelný trh, or follow Minoritská and Josefská southwards to the restored turn-of-the-century **railway station**.

Náměstí svobody (Liberty Square)

Hearty Czech cuisine

Other Places of Interest

◆◆
MORAVSKÉ GALÉRIE (MORAVIAN GALLERY)
Husová
Puropse-built towards the end of the 19th century by a Jewish philanthropist, the gallery houses superb displays of the applied arts from medieval times onwards, with a succession of rooms devoted to furniture, porcelain, glass and other decorative objects – one of the finest collections of its kind in Central Europe.

◆
MORAVSKÉ MUZEUM
Dietrichstein Palace and Bishop's Palace, Zelný trh
The prize exhibit of this museum's extensive natural history and archæological collections is the 25,000-year-old, flagrantly female figurine known as the Venus of Vestonice. The museum's ethnographical section, with fine folk artefacts, is in the northeast corner of Náměstí Svobody; the Technical Museum is on the corner of Josefská Street.

◆◆
ŠPILBERK
For centuries, Brno's hilltop citadel served as a prison for the enemies of Austria-Hungary, until its horrors were exposed by a former inmate, the 19th-century Italian rebel count Silvio Pellico. Later, the Gestapo used it to incarcerate and torture Czech patriots. All this can be relived in the course of a tour, though some of the interior is undergoing refurbishment to house the City Museum.

Practicalities

Accommodation
Astoria, Novobranská 3 (tel: 05 275 26). Central location. Budget.
Avion, Česká 20 (tel: 05 276 06). Fuchs' 1920s functional hotel. Moderate.
Brno, Horní 19 (tel: 05 63 900). Minimal modern suburban box, fine if you have a car. Moderate to expensive.
Slovan, Lidická 23 (tel: 05 74 54 55). Short tram ride north of centre. Moderate.

Restaurant
Černý mědvěd, Jakubske námestí (tel: 05 27 276). Intimate atmosphere and excellent specialities, including goose liver.

Pub
Špalíček, Zelný trh 12. Extremely popular with real beer drinkers, spilling out onto the cabbage market in fine weather. Hearty food.

WHAT ELSE TO SEE IN MORAVIA

◆◆
JAROMĚŘICE NAD ROKYTNOU

The little town square of Jaroměřice in southern Moravia is almost completely overwhelmed by a huge baroque palace, built in the early 18th century for the Questenburg family. The grand courtyard is matched in scale by the monumental oval church to the west and by the garden façade, staring out over the remains of an elaborate French style garden. The interior is equally ambitious, with elaborately decorated rooms and halls including a theatre and ancestors' hall. One of the Questenburgs, Count Johann Adam, was a great patron of music, and today the palace is the focus of an annual summer music festival.

◆◆◆
KROMĚŘÍŽ

From the 13th century on, the powerful bishops of Olomouc chose Kroměříž as their summer residence. Their palace was rebuilt many times; its latest, baroque face, capped by an earlier, 15th-century tower broods over the handsome main square, with its fine plague column in the middle and the tall town hall tower to one side.
The bishops lived in some style, as becomes apparent in the course of the guided tour around the palace interior. Their picture collection is one of the finest in the country, with paintings by Cranach, Titian, Van Dyck and many other old masters. They dispensed feudal justice from the Court Hall, with its superb ceiling frescos, and then partied in the immense Congress Hall. It was here, in 1848, that the Habsburgs bungled the last chance of preserving their decaying empire, when they had the mildly reformist Imperial Diet thrown out by the soldiery. Originally laid out in the French, formal manner, the grounds running from the palace to the river were re-landscaped in the early 19th century in the 'natural' English manner. But the **Květná zahrada (Flower Garden)** to the west is still in its original baroque state, with a huge central pavilion, radiating avenues of clipped hornbeam and a Roman colonnade of improbable length.
The streets of Kroměříž are pleasant to stroll in, with the prettiest houses running up Janská Street to the baroque Church of St John the Baptist. Back in the main square, the **Museum** has good local collections and a gallery devoted to one of the great Czech artists of recent times, Max Švabinský, who was born here in 1873.

Accommodation

Bouček, Velké náměstí 108 (tel: 0634 88147). Trim, clean, modern, on main square. Moderate.

◆◆
LEDNICE

The mighty Liechtenstein family rebuilt their Schloss on the Austro-Moravian border several times after it first came into their possession in the 16th century. The palace owes its present exuberant Gothic-cum-Tudor appearance to the efforts of their mid-19th century architect, who was sent to England to bone up on fashionable revivalist styles. The interiors are equally sumptuous, with numerous works of art; in addition, there is a museum of hunting, farming and forestry. The extensive **Landscape Park** is one of the finest in Central Europe, a fitting home for the landscape architecture faculty of Brno University. As well as fine specimen trees, lakes and islands rich in bird life, it has an array of garden buildings, mock castles, temples, a triumphal arch and even a minaret.

◆◆◆
MORAVSKÝ KRAS
(MORAVIAN KARST)

The action of water on this limestone massif north of Brno has produced a fascinating array of sink-holes, underground rivers, chasms and more than 400 caves, some with splendid displays of stalagmites and stalactites. Though some of this subterranean world remains unexplored, the more spectacular features are among the most popular tourist attractions in the whole country. The classic day's outing from Brno is to the **Punkevní jeskyně (Punkva Caves)**, involving not only caves and a boat trip on the underground Punkva River but also a view of the **Macocha Abyss**, a 453-foot (138m)-deep chasm which has sheer walls and rare vegetation.

◆◆◆
OLOMOUC ✓

On the upper reaches of the River Morava, old Olomouc claims more historic buildings than anywhere else in the country outside Prague, though the Old Town in which they stand has to be approached through the usual ring of grimy suburbs. The city lost its status as capital of Moravia to Brno after being sacked by the Swedes in the Thirty Years' War. The rebuilding which then took place gave the city its present handsome, mainly baroque face. Olomouc is also a university city, seat of an Archbishop, and the most important regional centre in Moravia apart from Brno and Ostrava. Until the early 1990s, a big Soviet garrison was stationed here; the farmers of the fertile Hana area to either side of the Morava are reputed to be the best-armed peasants in Europe, the soldiers of the Red Army having converted their lighter weapons into cash before leaving.

The ancient core of the city is around the much-restored **Cathedral of St Wenceslas (Sv Václav)**. Here, too, is the **Přemyslovský palác (Premyslid Palace)**; the area was settled by the Slavs as far back as the 8th century, and the Romanesque remains here are some of the most important in the country. Václavské náměstí (Wenceslas Square) is one of several nodal points in the Old Town, each ornamented by a fine fountain; along the tram lines to the west is Náměstí

Republiky (Republic Square), but the most important city space is the oddly shaped **Horní náměstí (Upper Square)**. Horní has two fountains – one for Hercules, one for Julius Caesar, Olomouc's legendary founder; these are upstaged, however, by the biggest, boldest and most superbly vulgar **Trinity Column** in the country. Even this has to compete for attention with the free-standing **City Hall**, built and rebuilt many times over since the 14th century; one side is adorned with an astronomical clock, whose original medieval figures (Death, Knight, Maiden etc) were destroyed in World War II and have been replaced by rather touching representations of the workers of the Communist era. Most of the streets in the Old Town have something to show; Dolní náměstí (Lower Square) has more fountains and a comparatively modest column, and the Church of St Maurice (Sv Moric) boasts the biggest organ in the Czech Lands. The city's baroque fortifications, which had long constricted its growth, gave way in the 19th century to new building and fine parks; this green heritage has helped make Olomouc the venue for the country's most extravagant garden festival, Flora Olomouc, which is held annually in May.

Accommodation
Flora, Krapková 34 (tel: 068 232 41). Expensive.
Národní dům, 8 května 21 (tel: 068 24 806). Central. Moderate.
Sigma, Jeremenková 36 (tel: 068 27 153. Close to station. Budget.

Restaurant
Hanácká, Dolní náměstí 38. Local dishes of the Hana area.

Julius Caesar's fountain, Olomouc

MORAVIA

OSTRAVA

Most visitors will find
themselves in this huge
industrial conurbation on
business rather than pleasure.
There are a few sights to be
seen; the central focus of the
city is formed by Masarykovo
náměstí (Masaryk Square), on
which stands the Stará radnice
(Old City Hall), housing the city
museum. There is a gallery with
good examples of 19th- and
20th-century Czech painting in
the Palace of Culture, and the
Gothic Church of St Wenceslas
has somehow survived the
centuries.

Once these possibilities have
been exhausted, there is fine
upland countryside to be hiked
through in summer and skied
over when snow is on the
ground. To the west are the
extensive **Jeseníky Mountains**,
reached from Ostrava via the
old textile and trading city of
Opava. Like Opava, the
Jeseníky were largely German-
speaking, and have never
regained their pre-war
population level, leaving parts
of the area with a rather forlorn
air. The highest point is Praděd,
topped by a TV tower; in the
valleys are resorts like Velké
Losiny, Karlová Studanka and
Lázně Jeseník, all of which have
seen better days but still retain
a faded charm.

To the south are the more
modest heights of the **Beskydy
(Beskids)**, where woodlands
alternate with high pastures,
and where there is a robust
heritage of building in timber.
Places to visit *en route* could
include Novy Jičín, with its

splendid old town square and
what is claimed to be the
world's only **Hat Museum**.
Kopřivnice is the home of Tatra,
the other (non-Skoda) Czech
motor works, with a museum
whose displays include the
firm's most famous vehicle, the
black saloon once used to ferry
Party functionaries around.

◆◆
PERNŠTEJN

Rising from a rocky spur among
the pinewoods, mighty
Pernštejn has everything a
feudal fortress should have:
sheer walls, projecting turrets
and windows, a wooden bridge
to span the abyss. The core of
the castle consists of a 13th-
century round tower, but over
the centuries the powerful
Pernštejn family and their
successors have added their
bits, giving the place its
appealingly irregular outline as
well as some strangely
incongruous rococo interiors.

◆◆
ROŽNOV POD RADHOŠTĚM
(ROZNOV UNDER RADHOST)

This valley town shelters
beneath the 3,704-foot (1,129m)
peak bearing the name of
Radhost/Radegast, a pagan
deity whose wooden effigy
guards the way to the chapel-
crowned summit. This part of
eastern Moravia was settled in
the late Middle Ages by Vlachs,
herdsmen from no-one knows
quite where. The timber-built
villages of the area demonstrate
the Vlachs' skills in advanced
carpentry, but the greatest
concentration of their work can
be seen at Roznov, where the

Skansen (Open-Air Museum)
is the largest and most
fascinating of its kind in the
country. The museum is in three
sections (with different opening
times), the Dřevené městečko
(Timber Village), with buildings
from towns and villages all
around, the Mlýnská dolina (Mill
Valley), with ponds and mill-
races driving the machinery
within an array of mill-buildings,
and the Valašská dedina (Vlach
Village), a reconstructed
version of a typical upland
settlement.

◆◆
SLAVKOV (AUSTERLITZ)
Not for nothing does a Paris
railway station bear the name of
this otherwise unpretentious
little place east of Brno, for it
was here on 2 December 1805
that Napoleon's army overcame
the numerically superior forces
of Russia and Austria. The
bloody encounter is known
hereabouts as the Battle of the
Three Emperors, since not only
the former Corsican corporal
but also Tsar Alexander and
Emperor Francis were present.
The battle was brought to a
formal end in negotiations held
in the town's huge baroque
castle, with its splendid central
hall and Napoleonic museum.
The many dead are
commemorated by a number of
striking monuments, of which
the most impressive is the
Mohyla míru; this extraordinary
Art Nouveau shrine, which has
been built in the form of an
ancient Slavonic burial place,
crowns the rise known as
Pratecky kopec, right in the
heart of the battlefield.

*Traditional beehives on display in
Rožnov Pod Radhoštěm*

◆◆◆
TELČ ✓

Telč is almost too perfect to be
true. From the castle at its
western end a beautifully
elongated main square opens
out, lined with arcaded town
houses, each topped with a
fanciful gable. Castle and town
were founded in medieval
times, on a spit of land standing
out from low-lying marshlands.
The watery surroundings were
turned to advantage,
transformed into a trio of great
ponds which not only added an
extra layer of defences to the
town walls, but also provided a
breeding-place for the carp so
much in favour in this land-
locked part of Europe. One
pond has disappeared, the
others remain.

The medieval castle was much extended in the later part of the 16th century, giving it a delightfully irregular layout. The interiors are outstanding, comprising some of the finest early Renaissance rooms in the country, The castle is linked by an arcade to the parish church, whose tower gives the best view down the length of the square towards the baroque column at the far end.

Telč is thankfully car-free, and must be approached on foot, best of all from the north through the Little Gate.

Accommodation
Černý Orel, one of the town's grander buildings, sited on the main square (tel: 066 962 221). Restaurant. Budget to moderate.

◆◆◆
VRANOV
This frontier castle, strung out along its rock spur high above the River Dyje, is one of the most stunning of Czech strongholds, a medieval fortress transformed in around 1700 by the great Viennese architect Fischer von Erlach into a sumptuous palace for the Althan family. The castle can only be approached on foot (a long walk up from the car park). Bridge and gatehouses lead to the central courtyard, with a giddy view of the village far below and of the ochre chapel clinging to the edge of the precipice. Upstaging all this scenic grandeur are the castle interiors, above all the extraordinary **Ancestors' Hall**, one of the great baroque spaces of Central Europe, a

Gabled houses line the splendid main square in Telč

glorification of the Althan clan in paintings, sculpture and triumphal architecture.

◆◆
ZLÍN
In the interwar period, this utopian factory town, built by the paternal boot and shoe manufacturer Bata, seemed to symbolise the liberal aspirations of the First Republic. Its architecture of red brick, glass and steel may now seem

dated, but only because it led to many, mostly inferior imitations. Laid out spaciously, with plenty of parks and gardens, it has the atmosphere of a spa rather than a workplace. The core of the town is around the factory (where there is a Shoe Museum), and the trio of functional civic buildings, store, hotel and cinema. From the glass pavilion called the Dům umění (House of Art), there is a view past the crisp housing blocks into the fresh Moravian countryside beyond.
Lesná Castle, 4 miles (7km)

northeast of Zlín, an exuberant late 19th-century Central European version of an English manor house, makes an enjoyable contrast to Zlín's functionalism. A zoo is installed in its park.

Accommodation
Garni, nám. T G Masaryka, Zlín (tel: 067 377 70). Fresh and modern, this is a better bet than the much more expensive Moskva next door (though the latter's French restaurant certainly deserves a visit). Budget to moderate.

EXCURSION INTO SLOVAKIA

Despite the split that took place on 1 January 1993, independent Slovakia will continue to be associated in the minds of many visitors with the Czech Republic, its partner for most of this century. No tourist trip was more exciting than the classic Czechoslovak itinerary taking in the urban delights of Bohemian Prague, then moving on to the raw peaks of the Slovak High Tatras. But Slovakia has more to offer than some of the continent's wildest mountain and forest scenery; ruled for a millenium by Hungary, settled by German miners and traders in the Middle Ages, the home of a pious peasantry, it boasts an impressive heritage of ancient towns, great fortresses and fine churches. There is no doubt that it will soon emerge as a tourist country in its own right, not least because of its accessibility (Bratislava is an hour's drive from Vienna).

BRATISLAVA ✓

From the upper windows of Bratislava's castle above the Old Town it is sometimes possible to pick out the skyline of Vienna, barely 30 miles (50km) away across the Danube Plain. Pressburg, as it is known in German, was very much a city of the Habsburgs; its Gothic cathedral was for centuries the place where these Emperors of Austria had themselves crowned as rulers of Hungary. The charming Old Town reflects this historic legacy, with its web of narrow street and intimate squares lined with fine town houses, unpretentious burghers' homes contrasting with the sumptuous palaces of the nobility. Since 1918 the principal focus of Slovak national life and now the fully fledged capital of an independent state, Bratislava seems destined to emerge from

Hviezdoslavovo náměstí, Bratislava

SLOVAKIA

SLOVAKIA EXCURSION – BRATISLAVA

the obscurity into which it fell when its tramway link to Vienna was cut by the Communists and when all the important decisions seemed to be made in Prague. An old city, struggling to maintain its crumbling heritage of ancient buildings and to overcome the problems of forced post-war growth period,

it is also the hopeful capital of a new-born state.

Places of interest

◆◆◆
BRATISLAVSKÝ HRAD (BRATISLAVA CASTLE)

The great rock rising abruptly over the fast-flowing Danube was settled by prehistoric

BRATISLAVA

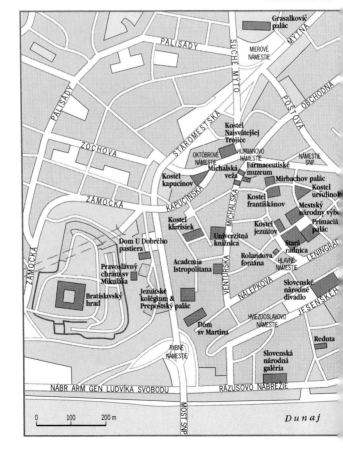

tribes, Celts, Romans, Slavs and Austrians. The forbidding fortress which now crowns the heights has been rebuilt several times, though its four-square plan dates from medieval times. Its plain appearance and prominent corner towers have led it to be referred to with wry affection as 'the upturned table'. The Slovak emblem flies from the high flagpole and soldiers

goosestep across the broad cobbled forecourt, reminders that this is now a centre of Slovak sovereignty, with Presidential quarters and reception rooms. It is also the home of many of the historical collections of the **Slovak National Museum**.

◆◆
DOM SV MARTINA (ST MARTIN'S CATHEDRAL)

The Gothic cathedral's steeply sloping roof, tall tower and spire make it an imposing landmark, guarding the approach to the Old Town from the modern SNP Bridge with a futuristic restaurant perched atop its pylons. The urban motorway leading north from the bridge almost clips the cathedral walls, demonstrating the former rulers' contempt for both history and religion, as well as cutting off the Old Town from the castle. Begun in the 14th century, the cathedral saw the crowning of no fewer than 11 Hungarian kings, as well as the first performance of Beethoven's *Missa Solemnis*.

◆◆
DOM U DOBRÉHO PASTIERA (THE HOUSE OF THE GOOD SHEPHERD)

Before the urban motorway to the Danube crossing smashed its way through the area at the foot of the castle hill, this rococo concoction of a house formed part of an intricate townscape of steep and cobbled streets teeming with activity. Inside the building, tortuous stairways lead through an array of rooms exclusively furnished with antique timepieces. Opposite, as the street named Zámocké schody begins its ascent towards the castle, another town house has been turned into a museum, furnished with local arts and crafts.

◆◆
HLAVNÉ NÁMĚSTIE (MAIN SQUARE)

Site of the medieval city market, this focal point of the Old Town has as its centrepiece the Renaissance Roland Fountain. The figure of Roland (who actually depicts the Austrian Emperor Maximilian II) is supposed to perform various antics at key moments of the year (like midnight on New Year's Eve), but these seem only to be visible to those prepared with adequate quantities of *slivovica*. Roland faces away from the fine Art Nouveau bank building (now housing one of the best cafés in town) towards the **Stará Radnïca (Old Town Hall)**, with its splendid medieval roof and high baroque tower. Beyond a vaulted passageway is a delightful Renaissance court-yard with arcading. Together with the adjoining Apponyi Palace, the Old Town Hall houses the **Mestké muzeum (City Museum)** with displays on city history and viticulture.

◆◆
HVIEZDOSLAVOVO NÁMĚSTIE (HVIEZDOSLAVOVO SQUARE)

This long, tree-filled square was laid out when the city's waterfront ramparts were demolished in the 18th century. A focal point of cultural life, it is terminated to the east by the flamboyant late 19th-century **Slovenské národné divadlo (Slovak National Theatre)**, while the most prominent structure to the south is the Carlton, one of the archetypal hotels of Central Europe. The square is named after the 'father of Slovak poetry', Pavolo Hviezdoslav.

◆
KAMENNÉ NÁMĚSTIE (STONE SQUARE)

Hardly beautiful, but always lively with trams and shoppers, this is one of the places where Bratislava begins to feel like a modern metropolis. The chunky Prior department store to the east is backed by the even chunkier Kiev Hotel, two enduring achievements of socialism, but perhaps more interesting is the Manderla building to the west, built in 1935 and one of the first high-rise structures to be found in Central Europe.

◆◆
MICHALSKÁ VEŽA (MICHAEL'S GATE)

The best way into Bratislava's Old Town is from Hurbanovo náměstí to the north. Opposite **Kostel Najsvátejsej Trojice (Trinity Church)**, perhaps the finest of the city's many baroque churches, a little bridge leads to the arch of this tall gateway topped by its statue of the Archangel Michael. The reward for a laborious climb up to the viewing gallery is a fine view over the old town. Southward from the tower Michalská (Michael's Street) runs into Ventúrska, both lined with venerable buildings and forming the heart of the university quarter.

◆

SLAVÍN

The forested heights of the Malé Karparty (Little Carpathians), their lower slopes one big vineyard, make a wonderful recreation area for Bratislava. High above the city is the Slavín Monument, one of the most elaborate of Soviet war memorials. To the west of the city, topping an isolated crag, is the ruined fortress of **Devín**, looking out from the confluence of the Danube and the Morava towards Vienna.

◆◆

SLOVENSKÁ NÁRODNÁ GALÉRIA (SLOVAK NATIONAL GALLERY)

Beyond the bold slab of modern building facing the Danube waterfront can be seen the main part of the National Gallery, an elegant 18th-century barracks. Colourful paintings by Slovak artists of the interwar period, such as Martin Benka, depict the traditional mountain life of central Slovakia.

Practicalities

Accommodation

Carlton, Hviezdoslavovo náměstie (tel: 07 58 209). Faded luxury in a Central European city centre hotel (possibly under reconstruction). Moderate.
Danube, Rybné náměstie 1 (tel: 07 34 00 00). Recently completed and still fresh, excellently located. Expensive.
Turist, Ondavská 5 (tel: 07 653 57). Basic but well managed accommodation among the

faceless flats near the Zimny štadión (Winter Sports Stadium) in the eastern suburbs; a swift tram ride into town. Budget.

Restaurants

Harmónie, Venturská 9 (tel: 07 33 16 83). Slovak specialities and attentive service in the heart of the Old Town. Budget.
Maďarská reštaurácia, Hviezdoslavovo náměstie 20 (tel: 07 334 883). Hungarian cuisine in spacious setting opposite the Carlton. Budget.

Cafés

Roland, Hlavné náměstie 5. High-ceilinged elegance in one of the best Art Nouveau buildings in town, a former bank.
U Liszta, Klariská 1. A cavernous bar with a large and leafy courtyard.

Pub

Stará sladovňa, Cintorínska 32. One of the biggest pubs in Central Europe, a beer hall know locally as 'Mamut' (mammoth), awash with Budvar and with deafening *dechová* (brass band) music.

Here for the beer

THE ROAD TO THE TATRAS ✓

The Danube flows eastward from Bratislava across a broad and fertile plain towards Budapest, on its way feeding the turbines of the controversial hydroelectric power station at Gabčikovo. Into the great river run a number of tributaries, like the Váh and the Hron, flowing from the mountainous northeast which constitutes the heartland of Slovakia. These highlands form part of the Carpathians, curving from Romania in a great protective arc around the Hungarian Plain and coming to a stop above Bratislava. In Slovakia they break down into a number of distinct massifs, where, among the upland pastures and dense forests of beech, spruce and fir, a rugged peasantry kept the Slovak soul alive throughout a thousand years of Hungarian rule. It was here that the 1944 Slovak National Uprising (SNP) took place, redeeming in many Slovaks' eyes the country's humiliating role as a puppet state of the Third Reich. Communism brought industry to the uplands, sometimes with unfortunate ecological consequences, but in the main the mountains have maintained their allure. Most spectacular are the **High Tatras**, a clutch of jagged peaks rising dramatically from forested lower slopes to form the frontier between Slovakia and Poland. From Bratislava, the main road and railway cross the Danube flatlands to join the valley of the River Váh, which penetrates the heart of the country via a succession of towns separated by constantly changing valley landscapes.

Medieval **Trnava**, only 28 miles (46km) from Bratislava, is still a city of the plain. With most of its walls still intact, it used to refer to itself as the Slovak Rome, trading on its ancient archbishopric and its many fine churches. The Váh is reached at **Piešťany**, the most important spa town in Slovakia, with a wealth of turn-of-the-century buildings. As the valley closes in, its strategic importance becomes more obvious; to the west is the first of many castles, ruined **Čachticky hrad**, residence of the notorious 'Blood Countess', Elizabeth Bathory. On the far bank is another mighty ruin, **Bečkov**, then, rising over the roofs and steeples of the old city of **Trenčíň**, an even more impressive stronghold, much

SLOVAKIA EXCURSION – THE ROAD TO THE TATRAS

restored, once the headquarters of the rebel aristocrat Matthias Čák. Beyond the industrial town of **Žilina** the river has cut through the Malá Fatra range to form a spectacular gorge. Among glorious beechwoods are the ruins of **Starý Hrad** (Old Castle) and, atop a crag, the great fortress of **Strečno**. The railway town of Vrútky marks the upstream entrance to the gorge, while just to the south is **Martin**, a stalwart centre of Slovak nationalism in the past and a sometime rival to Bratislava as Slovak capital. Here are the Slovak National Museum, with fascinating ethnographical collections, and a *skansen*, an open-air museum of Slovak timber buildings. The manor house in the village of Blatnica, further south, is now a museum devoted to the life and work of

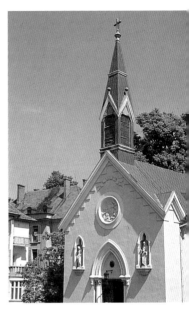

The spa town of Piešťany

THE ROAD TO THE TATRAS

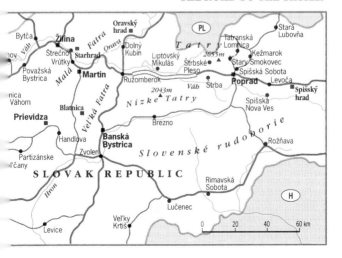

the greatest 20th-century Czechoslovak photographer, Karel Plicka.

Those who have acquired a taste for Slovak strongholds should divert from the Váh along the valley of the Orava to climb through keeps and courtyards to the dizzy lookout on which **Oravský hrad (Orava Castle)** was somehow constructed. South of the main route through Ružomberok and Liptovský Mikuláš are the **Nízké Tatry (Low Tatras)**, offering good skiing and walking.

The beauty, popularity and rich wildlife of the **High Tatras** led to their being declared a National Park in 1949. Relatively young mountains, mainly composed of granite, they have the highest peaks in the whole of the Carpathians; Gerlachovský Štít reaches 8,700 feet (2,655m) and Lomnický Štit 8,635 feet (2,632m). The bare rock of razor-edged ridges and giddy summits rises from glaciated valleys hiding scores of secret lakes. The gentler lower slopes carry a dense forest of spruce trees, the abode of lynx, wild cats, wolves and even bears. A panoramic road twists through the dark conifers, linking the three resorts of Štrbské Pleso, Starý Smokovec, and Tatranská Lomnica, and accompanied by a mountain railway which drops down to the main line at Štrba and Poprad. The latter town is the 'capital' of the Tatras, with stunning views northward of the main ridge. **Štrbské Pleso**, built around the lake of the same name, was the site of the World Alpine Ski Championships in

1970, and lost some of its character through the construction of some odd-looking hotels at the time. It's still dominated by the great ski-jump built for the occasion. **Starý Smokovec** has retained much of its charm, with timbered villas among the trees; **Tatranská Lomnica** is similar, with a bonus in the form of the modern and excellently laid out **TNP Museum** (Tatranský Narodni Park – Tatras National Park). A variety of transport – cable-car, funicular, chairlift – plus a network of footpaths (some sections closed during part of the year) are available, but your enjoyment may be diminished by crowds at high season. Mountain weather is notoriously fickle, and keen walkers should take all the usual precautions before setting off. When clouds obscure the mountains, you could do worse than explore the Spiš towns, founded by German merchants in the Middle Ages and mostly in a miraculous state of preservation. **Spišská Sobota**, in the suburbs of Poprad, **Kežmarok** (Käsmark) and **Spišská Nova Ves** (Zipser Neudorf) are all worth visiting, but the jewel among them is **Levoča** (Leutschau). Among the fine old houses in the main square is a Renaissance town hall and the parish church, the latter containing one of the great works of art of the Middle Ages, the limewood altar carved by Master Pavol. Further east are the ruins of the city-sized castle of **Spišský hrad**, dominating the countryside for miles around.

Peace and Quiet

*Countryside and Wildlife in the Czech Republic, including excursions into Slovakia
by Paul Sterry*

As the sun sets over the wooded slopes of the Tatras, a huge, ghostly shape glides from the cover of its cliff-face nesting site: an eagle owl, in search of its quarry of hares and small deer. The remote forests of the Tatras are among the last havens for these magnificent birds, along with many other upland and woodland species. For the visiting naturalist, the Czech Republic and Slovakia have much to offer. The wealth of plants and animals is a delight, whether you explore the forests and mountains or marshes and lowland plains.

Český kras (Bohemian Karst)

Limestone country to the south of Prague

The Bohemian Karst is an area of eroded limestone scenery forming pavements, gorges and caves. Explore the area between Beroun (on the E12) and the castle at Karlštejn. Limestone soils are extremely good for orchids, and a search among shady patches of woodland can often reveal military, monkey and lady's slipper orchids.

Limestone-loving military orchid

PEACE AND QUIET

Jeseníky Mountains
Mountain range on the Polish border

The Jeseníky Mountains lie roughly 93 miles (150km) due east of Prague and can be reached by driving to Hradec Králové and then on to Jeseník or Šumperk. The highest peak, Praděd, has a road giving access up to a considerable elevation; there is also a hotel below Praděd. The lower slopes of the mountains and hills

A great spotted woodpecker

The Great Bustard

The great bustard is the largest flying bird found in Europe. The size of a turkey, this shy bird is only found on wide open plains. Lowlands in the south of the Czech Republic and in neighbouring countries are among its last strongholds. A special reserve has been set up at Zlatná but great bustards can be seen almost anywhere in the region. If you are lucky enough to see one in flight, you will immediately notice the distinct black-and-white markings on the wings.

are cloaked in forest with broad-leaved species, such as beech, at lower elevations and conifers higher up. Above the tree-line, alpine grasslands harbour colourful flowers and breeding birds in the spring. There are upland lakes located near Rejviz.

Waymarked trails through the forests and hills provide an ideal way to explore the mountains; look out for woodpeckers and birds of prey, and for red squirrels and deer.

Jizerské Hory (Jizera Mountains)
Extensive mountain range centred on Jablonec nad Nisou and Liberec

The Jizera Mountains rise to a height of over 3,600 feet (1,100m) at Smrk, but in most areas are little over 1,640 feet (500m). Rivers and waterfalls cut into the landscape and the beech forests are among the finest in Central Europe.

Woodland Birds

Walks in the forests of the
Czech Republic are among
the highlights of any
naturalist's visit to the region.
Although a surprising amount
of woodland is in fact
plantation – planted after the
primary forest had been felled
– there are still plenty of
woodland birds to be seen.
Hazelhens and capercaillies
are both gamebirds found
living on the forest floor
throughout the year. Others,
such as flycatchers and
warblers, are summer visitors,
that arrive in April and May.
These are the months when
bird song is at its best.
Sometimes referred to as the
'dawn chorus', most singing
takes place just as the forest
gets light and a walk at this
time of day can be
memorable.

Krkonoše National Park (Giant Mountains)

*Forested mountains, northeast of
Prague on the Polish border*
The Krkonoše mountains which rise to over
5,000 feet (1,600m) on the
highest peak, Sněžka. The
lower slopes are mostly
covered with pine forests.
These give way, above the tree-
line, to areas of mountain
grassland. Hiking is a popular
pursuit here during the summer
months, particularly along the
border ridge from Sněžka to
Harrachov. Chairlifts, provided
for the use of skiers during the
winter months, can save hikers
a good deal of uphill leg-work.

Good access points to the
Krkonoše Mountains include
Lucní bouda in the east and
Horní Misecky in the west.
Visiting naturalists should look
for woodland birds such as
nutcrackers, woodpeckers and
tits, as well as mountain birds
including alpine accentors and
water pipits.

Lednické rybníky (ponds)

*Ponds and wetlands near the
Austrian border*
Lednické rybníky, 124 miles
(200km) southeast of Prague
and 31 miles (50km) south of
Brno, have been used to rear
carp for more than 500 years.
Minor roads between and
around the towns of Lednice
and Břeclav offer the best
means of exploring the area.
Stop in likely-looking spots with
open water, reed-beds or
scrubby wetland, and scan with
binoculars. During the summer
months, warblers, herons and
black kites are common and
white storks, which breed on
roofs in neighbouring villages,
visit the area. During migration
times – April to June and August
to October – the variety of birds
is greatest. Colourful wetland
plants flower in the spring and a
chorus of frogs sings out from
the vegetation.
Another area worth exploring
near by is made up of the
riverine forests and marshes
between Břeclav and Kuty, at
the confluence of the Rivers
Dyje and Morava, right on the
border. The largely
inaccessible terrain harbours
black woodpeckers, black
storks and many other wetland
and forest birds.

Novozamecký rybník (New Castle Pond)
Pond and wetlands, north of Prague

The reserve of Novozamecký rybník is roughly 31 miles (50km) due north of Prague near the village of Zahradky, close to Česka Lipa. Look for breeding birds such as herons, marsh harriers, black-headed gulls and red-crested pochards. Migrant birds, such as terns, waders and wildfowl, turn up in spring and autumn.

Orlické hory (Eagle Mountains)
Wooded mountains, southeast of Krkonoše

The Eagle Mountains are extremely popular with hikers and visitors keen on the

An edible frog soaks up the sun in a shallow stretch of water

The Edible Frog
Visit even the smallest water body in the spring and you are likely to see numerous pairs of beady eyes staring back at you. These probably belong to edible frogs that gather here to mate and spawn. To accompany their courtship, the males produce croaking calls to attract the attention of the female frogs. Edible frogs are beautifully marked with various shades of green and irregular brown and black blotches. They are rather nervous creatures and when frightened quickly swim to the bottom of the pond or lake.

outdoors. The forested slopes of the ridge are home to many birds of prey and woodland birds such as red-breasted

flycatchers and woodpeckers.
The administrative centre of the
region is Rychnov nad Kneznou.

Šumava Hills
*Wooded hills on the Bavarian
border*
The Šumava Hills lie along the
border with Germany and
Bohemia and are the watershed
for the Vltava. Forests of beech
and other broad-leaved trees
cover the lower slopes of the
hills and give way to conifers –
firs and spruce – at higher
elevations. The latter are home
to breeding crossbills and
redpolls. Above the tree-line
there are meadows and
grasslands full of flowers in
spring and summer. The
administrative centre is Sušice,
from where a road runs south
along the scenic valley of the
Vydra. The hills also harbour
the Czech Republic's largest
reservoir, Lipno Lake.

Třeboň
*Ponds and wetlands close to the
border between south Bohemia
and Austria*
Třeboň lies about 75 miles
(135km) due south of Prague
and is at the heart of a wetland
area harbouring a network of
former and current carp-
rearing ponds that are excellent
for water birds. Lakes Velký
Tisý, Malý Tisý and Rožmberk
are particularly good, and the
birds and other wildlife can be
seen from the road. Some of the
ponds have nature reserve
status and harbour grebes,
wildfowl, herons and egrets. As
well as the fish, for which the
ponds were created, toads,
dragonflies and other fresh-
water creatures thrive here.

*The remote forests of the Tatras
provide a haven for the eagle owl*

Excursion to Bratislava
*Slovak city with adjacent wetland
and agricultural lowlands*
Although Bratislava itself may
have limited wildlife interest,
the Danube lowlands have
farmland and lakes which are
worth a look. Explore the area
around Trnava, stopping to
scan the fields and the man-
made lakes that occur here and
there. Scan overhead wires for
great grey and lesser grey
shrikes, and for red-footed
falcons which nest in some of
the patches of woodland.
Penduline tits build their
suspended, flagon-shaped
nests in the willows that grow in
wetter areas and egrets, herons
and marsh harriers frequent the
watery margins.

PEACE AND QUIET

Excursion to the Tatra Mountains

Extensive mountain range in northern Slovakia

These dramatic mountains are a popular excursion from the Czech Republic. The High Tatras are surrounded by lower ranges and provide excellent opportunities for hiking and observation of wildlife. The headquarters of the national park are at Tatranská Lomnica and villages along the road from Ždiar to Strbské pleso make particularly good starting points for walks.

In common with other wooded areas in Central Europe, the forests on the lower slopes comprise mainly broad-leaved trees such as maple, ash, rowan and beech, whereas the more hardy conifers, including larch, spruce and fir, prevail at higher elevations. The woods harbour deer, wildcats and pine martens, all of which are rather secretive. Woodland birds such as capercaillies, warblers, flycatchers and woodpeckers are easier to see. Above the tree-line, the open mountain slopes are home to rock thrushes, golden eagles, ring

The High Tatras

ouzels and alpine accentors. On the northern slopes of the Lower Tatra Mountains is the Demanovská dolina (the Demanova Valley). This is karst country, with gorges, cliffs and caves containing fossil remains and stalactites.

To the south of the Tatra Mountains lies the Dobroc Forest, which cloaks the Slovenské Rudohorie (Slovak Ore Mountains) near Banksá Bystrica. A visit here can be included on a trip the the Tatras. The Hron Valley, which lies on the northern slopes, with the Lower Tatras to the north, is a good point from which to start hiking. Waymarked trails lead from Čierný Balog and Brezno. On the lower slopes, there are forests of ash, beech, maple and other broad-leaved trees. In the spring, listen for the wood warbler's trilling song, and look for flycatchers perched on bare branches. Several species of orchids grow here and fungi are abundant in the autumn. Higher up, the forests become dominated by conifers such as firs and spruce.

Practical

This section (with the yellow band) includes food, drink, shopping, accommodation, nightlife, tight budget, special events etc

FOOD AND DRINK

You are unlikely to go hungry in this country, though what you are offered will not always be easily reconciled with strict calorie control; meat (*maso*) and dumplings (*knedlíky*), bread (*chleb*) and cakes (*zákusky*) are in abundant supply; the difficulties start with salads (*salát*), fruit (*ovoce*) and fresh vegetables (*zelenina*). Like other Central European cuisines, Czech cooking is based on a relatively limited range of excellent ingredients and the need to fortify body and soul for hard work and cold winters. The pig (*vepř*) is king in the hierarchy of farm animals, accompanied by beef (*hovězí maso*) cattle, veal (*telecí maso*), chickens (*kuře*), geese (*hus*) and ducks (*kachna*). Fish is generally limited to trout (*pstruh*) or carp (*kapr*), hauled in tens of thousands from great fishponds in the south. The arable fields of the Labe valley supply grain for a bewildering variety of flour. Most of the root crops grown are sugar-beets, destined to fulfil the nation's need for sugar in its cakes, sweets and Turkish coffee.

In a (largely successful) attempt to neutralise political opposition, the post-1968 invasion government did its best to keep food shops full. Oranges and bananas may have been a rare luxury, but there were rarely shortages of traditional foods. Nowadays more or less everything is available (at a price), but eating habits have yet to change significantly. The greatest variety is likely to be found in small towns.

A Czech sausage shop

FOOD AND DRINK

At breakfast, eggs (*vejci*) in the glass or better still *hemenegz* (eggs and bacon, deliciously fried together) will set you up for the day. Bread will probably be rye, flavoured with caraway seeds. Coffee (*kava*) is likely to be of the Turkish type, good and strong, and fine as long as you don't try to drain the dregs! Tea (*čaj*) is always available too, but may be too weak for some tastes. It's better without milk. As the effects of breakfast begin to wear off, supplementary nourishment will be easy to find in the form of strong-tasting sausages (*párky*) dispensed from booths or snack-bars (*bufet*). Some of the best food in these latter establishments consists of a roll or slice of bread topped with combinations of salami, egg, mayonnaise and a gherkin (*okurka*), which can be accompanied by heavier forms of salad (potato, mixed vegetables).

As sightseeing begins to take its toll, drop into a café (*kavárna*) for coffee and a cake. Czechs are among the world's great patisseurs, their creations light, flavoursome and very tempting, worth indulgence even at the price of missing the evening meal. But you are unlikely to want to forgo this culinary high point of the day. Avoiding the often disappointing offerings of exotic (non-Czech) cuisines and go for local specialities. Soups (*polévky*), made from every conceivable ingredient, may turn out to be very filling. Leave

FOOD AND DRINK

room for the tender pork (*vepřové maso*) whose juices infuse the accompanying dumplings (*knedlíky*). More refined dishes might include goose liver (*husí jatra*) or carp (*kapr*) lightly stewed in white wine. Make up your mind not to be disappointed by the accompanying vegetables or salad, both likely to be nondescript, and make sure there is still some space for more dumplings, this time encasing wonderful sharp-sweet plums (*švestky*) or cherries (*třešně*). Strudels (*závin*) and pancakes (*palačinky*) are equally delicious options for dessert. Modern beer of the lager type

was invented and refined here, in Plzeň and elsewhere. No amount of expensive promotion of Czech-sounding names can disguise the wateriness of what passes for beer in much of the rest of the world, compared with the robust and toothsome liquid brewed in Bohemian (and Moravian) breweries. As well as the giants at Plzeň, Prague (Smíchov) and Budějovice (Budweis), many other towns have their own brands, usually with a distinct character. Not all Czech beers are lagers; few visitors to Prague miss a tasting of the dark brew prepared on the premises of one of the city's most famous pubs, U fleku.

A shady Prague café

Wine and spirits
Czechs love wine (*víno*). One of Europe's northernmost vineyards is at Mělník, down the Vltava from Prague, but most of the country's wine comes from warm lowlands of Moravia, along the Austrian border and the River Morava. Quality is variable, from very ordinary to excellent, and standards are expected to improve. Finally, for your aperitif or digestif, don't forget Karlovy Vary's 13th spring, Becherovka, fiery Borovicka or glorious plum-based *slivovice*.

In rapidly changing times, the restaurant (*restaurace*) scene is confusing. Outside Prague, the traditional place to eat was the hotel, and this is still true of many places. Bigger hotels may have more than one restaurant. The menu (*jídelní lístek*) may

Bohemian porcelain – a good buy

look long, but the real variation may only be in the meats, served up with the same array of vegetables. Non-hotel restaurants are likely to be more expensive, especially those in Prague, where rates are charged which very few locals can afford.

Vegetarians

In Prague, the Vegetarka restaurant on Celetná ulice serves some vegetarian food, but generally vegetarians should stock up on ingredients from shops whenever possible. Even omelettes are often served up with ham (*sumka*) unless you specifically demand otherwise. Fish-eaters have the additional option of carp and trout on many menus.

SHOPPING

Several years on from the downfall of Communism and the opening of the frontiers, many goods from all over the world are available in the Czech Republic, at world prices. There are modest displays in shop windows of the products of the international consumer society, from computer games and hi-fi systems to kitchen equipment. The snag is that most local wages and salaries are still a long way behind those in the West, and that something like a state-of-the-art TV set will eat up the equivalent of several months' wages.

Not least because of the modesty of local incomes, many everyday items still cost much less than their equivalents abroad, although they are steadily catching up. A walk around a department store such as Prior or Kotva in Prague will be enough to convince most people of this. Not a few Austrians pop over the border to buy things like food, linen or garden tools.

Bohemia and Moravia have long been famous for their classic souvenirs; the previous regime always ensured these were available for visitors in the special hard currency stores trading under the Tuzex banner. They include Bohemian glass and crystal in both traditional and modern patterns, blood-red garnets and costume jewellery and porcelain (especially in the classic onion pattern). You might also be tempted by craft items like lacework and textiles, metal and wooden objects, ceramics, prints and paintings. Some of these will be found in the craft shop called Dilo. Books and recorded music are in plentiful supply, many of the former being published in a range of languages. Illustrated books and children's books are often of very high quality. Second-hand bookshops may be worth a browse for maps, prints and ephemera as well as for books in a language you understand. Recordings are often first rate, especially the Czech 'greats', but you might like to listen to some local pop, as well as the ubiquitous *dechovka*, the brass band sound with plenty of oomph.

Until 1989, virtually all shops were nationalised and traded under inspired names like Maso (meat), Knihy (books), or Potraviny (foods). They made little attempt to entice customers to buy; in fact the customers had to take the initiative, for example in finding out when the delivery of a rare item (like oranges) was to take place. You may still come across unreconstructed shop assistants who regard customers with indifference if not hostility. The 'Little Privatisation' has resulted in many of these outlets passing into private hands and there is a growing number of new shops, most noticeably in Prague. Markets are popular and a good source of fresh fruit and vegetables. Prague has a western-style supermarket in yp, Senová 2232, Prague 4, Metro Chodov.

ACCOMMODATION

Like all other aspects of national life under Communism, accommodation in hotels and elsewhere was provided according to a plan. This left most towns with a limited range of places to stay, at least one of which would also act as a social centre with a variety of facilities – a restaurant (or two), bar, night-club and so on. Many historic buildings in town centres were adapted in this way, while others were purpose-built, usually in the prevailing heavily modern style. Many such places offered a lower standard of comfort than might have been expected from their rating. Some have been closed, others continue to operate much as before, and many are being privatised and renovated.

This somewhat shopworn heritage is now being supplemented by an increasing number of new, private establishments, sometimes in converted buildings, sometimes in purpose-built structures. Grading of hotels is now normally by star rating (from ***** = international luxury standard to * = modest). An increasingly popular alternative to hotels is bed and breakfast in a private home, obviously variable in quality, and usually announced by the German sign *Zimmer frei*. Camping (*Autokempink*) is well developed and very economical, with facilities ranging from the most basic (toilets and a tap) to elaborately laid out sites with shops and a

ACCOMMODATION

The Moskva hotel, Zlín

bar, and the possiblility of staying in a chalet as an alternative to your tent.

There is an acute shortage of hotel accommodation in Prague and the spa towns tend to fill up, too. Brno is packed when trade fairs are held, as are the winter sports resorts in the Giant Mountains. Advance booking in these cases is definitely advisable. In other places the risk of not being able to find accommodation is generally fairly low.

A number of agencies handle private rooms in Prague. Elsewhere you could try local Cedok offices, or simply keep your eyes open for the *Zimmer frei* sign. If you look like a lost tourist, especially at a main railway station, you may be approached by someone with a room to let. Make sure you check carefully on price and location before setting off.

Costs

A dual charging system operates in many establishments. Few Czech citizens are able to afford international rates and are therefore granted concessions, which are likely to be a fraction of what visitors from abroad will be asked to pay. This is not a scam, but a logical response to the economic situation. Rates for luxury hotels are set at an international level, and in Prague even hotels offering very modest standards of comfort and service may seem expensive. Outside the capital, prices are variable, and there are often bargains to be had as well as some nasty surprises. The cost of breakfast will not normally be included, unless you are staying in a private room.

CULTURE, ENTERTAINMENT AND NIGHTLIFE

Czechs have always produced disproportionate numbers of musicians and composers. Folk music formed a solid foundation for the achievements of classical masters like Dvořák and survived in spontaneous form until quite recently. It's now conscientiously preserved by local enthusiasts and by well-resourced (until recently at least) groups of the national ensemble type. A Moravian village band is likely to feature violins, a double bass, clarinet and cimbalom, while the bagpipes of a group from Domazlice in the far west of Bohemia are bound to get your feet tapping. Brass bands play in parks or dance halls; every factory seems to support one of these, belting out immortal oompah hits like *Skoda lásky*, the prewar number composed by the doyen of *dechovka* (as his music is known), Jaromir Vejvoda. You may know it better under its English title of *Roll Out The Barrel*. Take the opportunity to go to the opera or to a classical concert featuring the work of some of the country's great composers. A visit to Prague's National Theatre is an experience in itself, and while many concert halls are closed in the summer months there are many open-air performances to compensate (see **Special Events**).

Pop music is mostly derivative, though local traditions have influenced figures as diverse as Karel Gott, 'The Golden Voice from Prague' and the rock group Plastic People of the Universe.

The formerly state-supported Czech cinema (*kino*) has produced many fine films, some of which have become international classics (*A Blonde in Love, Closely Observed Trains*). Times are harder now, and the industry's future is uncertain. Foreign films were almost always dubbed into Czech with great skill, but this was expensive, and the cheaper alternative of sub-titling is now becoming more widespread. Animated films occupy a niche of their own, with practitioners like Jan Švankmajer enjoying a worldwide reputation.

The Laterna Magica of Prague is an inventive and highly entertaining multi-media show

Music is never in short supply

(acting, mime, film), requiring no knowledge of Czech and consequently extremely popular with tourists.

Nightlife in the form of clubs, bars and floor shows is much more developed in Prague than anywhere else. The biggest concentration of late-night activity is around Wenceslas Square; elsewhere, night owls hang around in bars (*vinarna*), which are frequently attached to the main hotel in town.

Listings appear in the weekly *Prague Post*, and there is an English language monthly, *Prague Guide*, plus weekly/monthly directories published in Brno and Bratislava. Tickets for theatre and opera performances should be obtained well in advance if possible, via your hotel desk, directly at the box office or in Prague through Prague Information Service, Na Příkopě 20, Praha 1 (tel: 02 54 44 44).

WEATHER AND WHEN TO GO

The Czech Republic is situated on the borderline between two great climatic regimes, the oceanic and the continental, and weather consequently tends to be fairly variable.

The country's mountainous rim catches the clouds generated by the Atlantic and rainfall here is quite high; the compensation is reasonably reliable cover of snow, with the highest peak in the Giant Mountains, Sněžka, having an annual average of 130 days of snowfall.

The interior of the country, particularly the lowlands around Prague and the lower Labe and southern Moravia, has much lower rainfall and higher temperatures generally, with warm or hot summers interrupted by thunderstorms.

Violin recital, gypsy-style

Winter days and nights can be cold and termperature inversions are common, with unpleasant conditions arising when air pollutants are trapped. Another area which has been badly affected in this way is the north Bohemian brown coal basin, where the contaminants produced by lignite-fired power stations create dangerous levels of air pollution if they are not dispersed by wind action.

Short days and the closure of many provincial museums and historic buildings are a deterrent to touring the countryside in winter, but the cultural life of cities flourishes at this time and there may be less pressure on accommodation. Spring can be late in starting, but when it arrives parts of the countryside are glorious with the blossom of fruit trees. In the summer months Prague in particular fills to the brim with foreign tourists and elsewhere there may be less choice of accommodation.

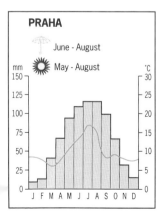

HOW TO BE A LOCAL

The westernmost of all the Slav peoples, the Czechs have mingled with their neighbours for long enough for their way of life to be characteristically Central European. Occasional echoes of Habsburg style, like elaborate deference to women and insistence on the use of titles like 'doctor' and 'professor' have been overlaid by 40 years of Communist egalitarianism. Nobody is called comrade (*soudruh*) anymore, but you may still come across some good old-fashioned indifference to the customer when shopping or eating in a restaurant. This is nothing personal, merely a product of the former system, and certainly not typical of the Czechs, who on the whole are helpful, kind-hearted people.

Compared with their Polish cousins, the Czechs might be said to lack a certain dash. They are ironic rather than fiery, prone to a quiet joke rather than a passionate speech. History has drilled into them the virtues of patience, of quietly subverting the system rather than confronting it head-on. Getting to know Czechs is not difficult. Once a certain initial reserve has been overcome you will find them both communicative and hospitable. They will be interested to hear about your experiences in their country and may well want to help you enjoy your stay more by giving you good advice, showing you round, even inviting you home. Don't take this for granted though, and

HOW TO BE A LOCAL

Rooftop greeting in Prague

remember that life is still more difficult and expensive for most people here than it is for tourists. Any gesture you might make, for example by offering flowers or issuing a reciprocal invitation, will be warmly received. In spite of the prevalence of second homes in the countryside, there is an acute housing shortage. It's rare for young people to be able to set up on their own, the norm being to spend the first few years of married life with one or other of the couple's parents. However daunting the language may look, it's worthwhile learning a few words and expressions. Russian lessons used to be compulsory in schools, but German is the main language of tourism and commerce, with English enjoying a certain prestige among the young because of pop culture.

Fenced off from a wider world and unable to articulate their real opinions for 40 years, Czechs regard their future with a mixture of hope, apprehension, and confusion. Some are embracing every aspect of Western culture with unthinking admiration, others see old certainties crumbling and are only too ready to look for scapegoats. Expect to find attitudes expressed which don't conform to what is regarded as 'politically correct' in the West.

CHILDREN

Quite an elaborate infrastructure was developed under Communism to cater for children's needs, from the cradle onwards. Every enterprise had its crèche, Young Pioneers had their camps and crocodiles of brightly dressed children were continually on the move on educational outings of one kind or another. This is changing, not necessarily for the better. In general Czechs are well-disposed towards children, though older people will often reproach them for 'outrageous' behaviour in public which might be tolerated at home. Certain aspects of the country are sufficiently 'different' to amuse and stimulate children from some Western countries, like riding round a city aboard a tram or taking a tiny train up a branch line. Tried and tested attractions include zoos (Troja in Prague, Lešná near Zlín), and the technically minded will enjoy the Museums of Technology in Prague and Brno. There are open-air events all over the country in summer, some of which will appeal to young people, while every town of any size has a park. The puppet theatres in Prague are almost bound to please. Nowadays virtually any product can be obtained, but unusual items may take some time to track down. If your child has any special requirements, you may want to provide for them before you leave. Big hotels may be able to arrange baby-sitting facilities.

TIGHT BUDGET

You can easily spend a lot of money in the Czech Republic by behaving like an international tourist, staying in four- and five-star hotels, amusing yourself in the nightclubs, eating in swish restaurants and taking guided tours around the sights. The economical – and usually enjoyable – alternative is to adopt native habits.

● Stay in private rooms or hostels (where they are available), or in a camp.

● Make up your mind to enjoy the (usually excellent) pork and dumplings and follow the local crowd into the ordinary restaurant or stand-up canteen. Try eating the delicious open sandwiches in the delicatessen (*lahudky*) or, alternatively, put together your own meal from the ingredients which are on sale there.

● Enjoy your evenings out in the pub (*pivnice*), or in the wine-bar (*vinárna*) of the local hotel.

● The entrance fee to most attractions is still generally quite low, so plan your own sightseeing itinerary, rather than put yourself into the hands of a tour operator.

● Make use of the public transport, which is remarkably cheap and will get you anywhere (given time).

● Do your souvenir-hunting in department stores, record and book shops rather than at the tourist traps.

SPECIAL EVENTS

Easter Girls and women are 'beaten' with willow switches and sprayed with water, and then present men with decorated Easter eggs.
Whit Sunday 'Ride of Kings' procession takes place in south Moravian villages.
May/June Prague International Spring Music Festival. Major event with performances of music, opera and ballet in various prestige locations.
June Kmoch Brass Band Festival, Kolin.
Late June Folk Festival, Strakonice, southern Bohemia.
Late June/early July International Folk Festival, Strážnice, southern Moravia.
July International Film Festival, Karlovy Vary (biennial, held in even years).
July/August Summer concerts held in Jaroměřice Castle, southern Moravia.
Mid-August Folk Festival of the Chod ethnic group, Domažlice, western Bohemia.
Mid-September Hop Festival, Žatec, northern Bohemia.
September Bagpiper Festival, Strakonice, southern Bohemia (biennially in even years).
October International Music Festival, Brno.
Velká Paradubická (Grand Steeplechase), Pardubice.
December 'St Nicholas', accompanied by an angel and a devil, roams the streets on the eve (5 December) of his saint's day. Live carp sold on street for Christmas Eve dinner. Christmas trees set up in town squares, decorated cribs arranged in church.

Czech festivities

SPORT AND LEISURE

As Czechoslovakia, the country was well known for excellence in a number of sports like tennis and ice-hockey. Facilities for most sports and outdoor activities are available, based in part on fine natural resources of rivers, mountains and uplands and on man-made features like major reservoirs.

Angling
With no ocean to fish in, Czech anglers make the most of the abundant streams, rivers and ponds which are systematically managed and replenished. Species include common trout,

rainbow trout, grayling and Danube salmon, sheatfish, carp, pike, pike-perch and tench.

Climbing
The sandstone cliffs of the Český ráj (Bohemian Paradise) and České Švýcarsko (Bohemian Switzerland) are good for climbing practice, but the real challenges are to be had in the high mountain country of Slovakia.

Football
Probably the country's most popular spectator sport, soccer pulls in the crowds at big stadiums like Dukla Praha and Sparta Praha. Tickets are cheap and usually available without problems at the gate before the start of a match (Sunday afternoons).

Golf
Golf is increasing in popularity, but as yet there are few courses (eg in Mariánské Lázně, Karlovy Vary, Poděbrady and at Motol in the Prague suburbs).

Motor-racing
Opened in 1987, the Masaryk Circuit outside Brno is the scene in August of the Motorcycle Grand Prix.

Rambling
Thousands of kilometres of waymarked routes criss-cross the country, with particular concentrations in areas of natural beauty. The 1:50,000

SPORT AND LEISURE

hiking maps with a key in English published by Klub Českých Turistu show the routes in detail.

Tennis

The Communist state's promotion of tennis helped produce household names like Lendl and Navrátilová, and the country is reasonably well-equipped with tennis courts, many attached to hotels.

Watersports

Most of the country's big reservoirs, like the Lipno dam in southern Bohemia, Slapy and Orlík south of Prague, and Vranov in southern Moravia, are used for watersports of all kinds. Most towns have covered swimming pools.

Winter Sports

Czechs are very keen on winter sports (Slovaks even more so) and head for the slopes whenever possible, putting a lot of pressure on facilities. The main ski areas (downhill and cross-country) are the Giant Mountains and the Jizera Mountains in northern Bohemia, the Ore Mountains in northwestern Bohemia and the Šumava in southwestern Bohemia, all equipped with lifts and trails. The very best skiing is in the Slovak mountains, above all among the superb scenery of the High Tatras.

Tennis: a national sport

Directory

This section (with the biscuit-coloured band) contains day-to-day information, including travel, health and documentation

Contents

Arriving

Passports and Visas

For citizens of most European countries, the US and Canada, a full passport (valid for at least three months after entry) is all that is required to enter the Czech Republic. Citizens of most other countries will require a visa as well, obtainable in advance at Czech embassies abroad or on the spot at a limited number of frontier crossings.

By Air

Some 12 miles (20km) west of the city centre, Prague's Ruzyně airport has direct flights to many European cities as well as to the US and Canada. London (Heathrow) to Prague takes two hours. There are internal connecting flights to Brno, Ostrava, Karlovy Vary and to various destinations in Slovakia including Bratislava and Poprad (for the High Tatras). Terminal facilities are underdeveloped. Connections to the city centre are by taxi, by airport bus direct, or by service bus to Dejvická Metro station and thence by Metro.

By Rail

The Czech Republic can be

DIRECTORY

On guard for the Czech railway

reached from all neighbouring countries by train. International expresses link Prague with Dresden and Berlin (via Děčín), Nuremberg, Frankfurt and Munich (via Plzeň), Vienna (via Tábor), Bratislava and the Tatras, and Budapest and Warsaw, and there is a service to and from Paris (via Plzeň). Local services cross the frontier at various points, linking Linz in Austria with České Budějovice in southern Bohemia, for example. Most international trains use Prague's Hlavní nádraži (Main Station), but some services may stop at suburban stations (Smíchov, Holešovice) which have a Metro connection to the city.

By Bus

There are international express coach services linking Prague with neighbouring countries as well as with London (about 24 hours one way). Journey times compare favourably in many cases with rail, and tickets are relatively inexpensive. For details of the Prague–London service call the operators, Kingscourt Express (Prague tel: 02 499 256; London tel: 081 769 9229) or Adco Travel (Prague tel: 02 683 0429; London tel: 071 372 0323).

By Car

The Czech Republic is not yet connected to the Western European motorway network, though plans are well advanced to fill the gap between the end of the Prague–Plzeň dalnice and the Autobahn in Bavaria. Since 1989, the limited number of main road border posts has been supplemented by the opening up of many minor road crossings which had been closed for 40 years. These can be handy at peak times when delays occur at some of the more important crossings, but check beforehand whether their use is restricted to the citizens of adjoining countries; some may only be open to pedestrians or cyclists.

Camping

Camping is very popular in the Czech Republic and there are sites in most parts of the country with concentrations in the more scenically attractive areas. Some are open all year round, but most operate between May and the beginning of October. They are graded into four categories from one star ('basic') to A and B (with showers and possibly other facilities, including chalets).Čedok offices should be able to provide a brochure detailing current facilities.

Car Rental

Car rental facilities exist in major centres and at Prague airport. Costs are not cheap, but always check whether any special offers are available. Most of the larger international operators are represented and local firms include Czech Auto Rent. Vienna is a good starting point for exploring Moravia; of the firms operating from the airport there, Europcar is used to its customers touring in the Czech Republic. No Austrian VAT is payable on mileage clocked up outside Austria.

Crime

One of the most bitter disappointments following the fall of Communism has been the increase in crime, from pickpocketing to smuggling of radioactive materials. Nevertheless, the level of crime is no worse than in most Western countries, and much less than in some. Take normal precautions like removing tempting objects from your car and locking it. Leaving your car in a supervised car park is a sensible precaution. Guard against pickpockets, particularly in places where tourists congregate. Remember that the standard of living which you take for granted may be the

subject of envy for people who earn perhaps a tenth of your income. It is normal practice for foreigners to be charged more than Czechs for their hotel room, but it's worth checking your bill in restaurants and elsewhere.

Customs Regulations
Arriving in the Country

The general principle is that you can bring into the country objects and articles for your personal use during your stay without paying duty. This includes 250 cigarettes or tobacco equivalent, up to 2 litres of wine and a litre of spirits. Modest gifts may be brought in up to a value which fluctuates but which is not usually likely to exceed a few thousand crowns.

Leaving the Country

Souvenirs up to a value of 50 per cent of the money you have exchanged into Czech crowns can be exported duty-free (more stringent regulations apply to day or weekend trippers). It's therefore necessary to keep all receipts. Articles bought with hard currency are free of duty. Many articles, like antiques, may not be exported without special permission.

Disabled Visitors

There are few special facilities in and around buildings and on public transport, and though the situation is likely to improve, in the near future the Czech Republic remains a less than ideal holiday destination for disabled people.

DIRECTORY

Driving

No special documentation is necessary for drivers bringing their own vehicles into the Czech Republic, though the vehicle registration book is officially required. If the vehicle's owner is not travelling, written permission from the owner is required. Green card insurance cover is advisable, as is an international driving licence.

Roads

The network of roads is dense and reasonably well maintained. The basic framework still consists of well-engineered but sometimes crowded single carriageways, but a motorway links Prague, Brno and Bratislava and there are other sections of motorway or dual carriageway, particularly radiating from Prague. Minor roads may be narrow and twisting.

Traffic Regulations

Drive on the right and overtake on the left. Safety belts must be worn and children under 12 years old must not sit in a front seat. Drinking and driving is absolutely forbidden, and infringements carry heavy penalties. Accidents causing personal injury or serious damage to a vehicle must be reported to the police. Vehicles must show an international identity sticker or plate, and carry a first aid kit and a red warning triangle and replacement bulbs. Don't compete with trams, which have their own traffic signals. At tram stops without central refuges, you must give way to passengers boarding and leaving the tram.

Speed Limits
In built-up areas: 60kph (37mph)
Motorways: 110kph (68mph)
Elsewhere: 90kph (56mph)

Parking

Parking is strictly controlled. Substantial parts of town centres and shopping streets are pedestrianised or closed to private traffic. Parking is not allowed at road junctions and pedestrian crossings or on a yellow line or where there is a No Parking sign (irrespective of the latter's visibility or lack of it). Policemen often lie in wait for cars infringing the rules and can extract a fine of a few hundred crowns. If in doubt, find a car park.

Fuel

Petrol and diesel are fairly widely available throughout the country, as is lead-free fuel, identified by the green sign Natural or by the German name *bleifrei*, but gaps between filling stations tend to be longer than in Western Europe and you should expect to queue occasionally. Most filling stations close at around 20.00hrs, and some may be closed on Saturday and Sunday, but there are some 24-hour facilities on motorways and on city approach roads.

Breakdown Services

Phone 154 for emergency breakdown service, and on motorways use the telephones provided. Alternatively contact the local Silniční služba (Road Service), whose telephone numbers are given in a brochure available at the frontier (in the Brno area, tel: 05 27 822, in the Plzeň area tel: 019 37 851). Letters of credit issued by your motoring club are accepted in the Czech Republic.

Electricity

220 volts, 50 cycles AC normally supplied to appliances via standard continental European two-pin plugs. Appliances fitted with three-pin plugs will require an adaptor; US appliances need a transformer, though hotel shaver points may be compatible.

Embassies and Consulates

Australia Praha 6, Čínská 4 (tel: 02 311 0641)
Canada Praha 6, Mickiewiczová 6 (tel: 02 312 0251)
UK Praha 1, Thunovská 14 (tel: 02 53 3347)
US Praha 1, Tržiště 15 (tel: 02 53 6641)

Emergency Telephone Numbers

Ambulance	155
Police	158
Fire Brigade	150
Road Accidents	154

Health

No special precautions are necessary, though if you have favourite remedies or drugs you may want to bring a full supply with you. People with respiratory problems might want to think twice about visiting Prague or certain industrial areas in the winter, when air pollution regularly reaches unpleasant or even dangerous levels.
Emergency treatment is free for

Making music

visitors from abroad. Further treatment is free for British citizens, who benefit from a reciprocal agreement between governments. But it's probably wise to take out medical insurance in case you need to be repatriated without fuss. People with health problems might like to consider a stay in one of the country's many spas, which between them are able to treat most conditions. The travel bureau Balnea (Praha 1, Pařížská 11, tel: 02 232 3767) specialises in arranging 'cures'.

Holidays
1 January – New Year's Day
Easter Monday
1 May – Labour Day
5 May – Anniversary of the Prague Uprising
8 May – Liberation from German occupation
5 July – Saints Cyril and Methodius
6 July – Anniversary of the burning at the stake of Jan Hus
28 October – Independence Day
1 November – National Holiday of Slovak Republic
24 December – Christmas Eve
25/26 December – Christmas holiday

Lost Property
In Prague, try the lost property office at Bolzanová 5, Praha 1 (tel: 02 236 8886). Elsewhere the police may be able to help.

Media
Newspapers and Periodicals
A good selection of international newspapers and periodicals can be found at kiosks in major cities. The local English-language *Prague Post* is published weekly and is useful for listings. It is resolutely North American in flavour, catering for the influx of young US citizens to Prague.

TV and Radio
The third TV channel transmits CNN at certain times of the day and night. The more expensive hotels have pay TV with programmes in foreign languages. Pop radio stations are proliferating.

Money Matters
The Czech unit of currency is the crown (Kč), divided into a hundred hellers (h), the latter being more of a hindrance than a help since they are practically valueless. The currency is not fully convertible, and you are not allowed to import or export it. If you wish to change crowns back into a convertible currency, make sure you keep the original receipts. As the Czech Republic separated from Slovakia, all banknotes except those for 10 and 20 crowns had to be handed in and stamped to retain their validity. Stamped Slovak crowns are no longer valid in the Czech Republic. The stamping was an interim measure; the old Czechoslovak crowns are being replaced by purpose designed Czech notes and coins, the first of which to appear were a Kč 200 note and a Kč 50 coin. Otherwise there are coins to the value of 10, 20 and 50 hellers, 1, 2, 5, 10 and 20 crowns, and notes to the

value of 100, 500 and 1,000 crowns.

Most banks change money – look for the sign saying *směnárna*. Commissions are modest, but the rarer foreign currencies may not be acceptable - this has been known to include sterling in remoter places. Black market money-changers used to patrol the streets and accost likely-looking foreigners. This is an unlikely experience nowadays, but don't be tempted if it does happen; you are likely to end up with a 'sandwich', with valid currency as the bread and unstamped or otherwise worthless notes or even lavatory paper as the filling. It's illegal too. There are more and more private enterprise *bureaux de change*, whose commission charge is likely to be higher than that of a conventional bank.

Credit cards are in increasing use, but outlets accepting them are still not widespread. The same applies to Eurocheques.

Opening Times
Banks
From Monday to Friday, usually 08.00–12.00hrs. Some banks reopen from 13.30 to 15.30hrs. City centre branches may have a more liberal opening regime.

Food Shops
Opening possibly as early as 06.00hrs, closing at 18.00hrs and 07.00hrs–midday on Saturday.

Other Shops
From 08.00 or 09.00hrs until 18.00 or 19.00hrs or between

Prague's Old Town Hall clock

midday and 14.00hrs on Saturday. Department stores may stay open until 16.00 on Saturday. There may be late night shopping on Thursdays (until 20.00hrs). The habit of closing without warning for weeks on end for *inventura* (stock-taking) seems to be on the wane. A few shops are now opening on Sunday.

Museums, Galleries and Historic Buildings
Tuesday to Sunday 10.00 to 17.00hrs. Many historic buildings are closed from November to March and may have restricted opening hours in April and September. As well as being closed on Mondays, some establishments may close on the day following an official holiday. Check in advance before setting off.

DIRECTORY

Offices
Monday to Friday
08.30–17.00hrs.

Post Offices
Monday to Friday
08.00–19.00hrs, to midday on
Saturday. The main post office
in Prague, at Jindřišská 14, is
open 24 hours.

Pharmacies
Identified by the sign Lékárna,
pharmacies stock a range of
drugs and medicines and may
be able to offer help in the case
of minor afflictions. Opening
hours correspond to those of
non-food shops. There are 24-
hour pharmacies in Prague, and
every pharmacy when closed
posts details of others which are
open at night and at weekends.

Places of Worship
A certain revival of religion has
taken place since 1989, but
Czechs generally are known for
their religious scepticism
(unlike the more devout
Slovaks) though most people
are nominally Roman Catholics.
Services in English are held in
Prague at the following
churches:
Anglican Church of St Clement
(Sv Kliment), Klimentská, Praha
1; Sunday 11.00hrs.
Church of Scotland Husová
kaple, Korunni 60, Praha 2;
Sunday 11.00hrs.
Roman Catholic Church of St
Joseph (Sv Josef), Josefská 4,
Prague 1; Sunday 10.30hrs.
Ecumenical International
Church (Cirkev bratrská),
Vrazová 4, Prague 5; Sunday
11.15hrs.
Outside Prague, you may find
churches closed when a
service is not being held.

Police
The national police (*policie*) are
identified by their khaki
uniforms and green and white
cars. The force no longer
occupies the commanding
position it enjoyed pre-1989,
and sometimes seems
overwhelmed by the
subsequent increase in crime.
Officers are generally very
courteous and helpful to visitors
from abroad. They are now
supplemented by municipal
police known as 'black sheriffs'
because of their intimidating-
looking black uniforms. Some of
these are recruited by security
companies such as Pinkertons
and enjoy only limited
confidence among the public.

Post Offices
The main *pošta* is likely to be an
important-looking building in
the centre of town. It is not the
only source of stamps (*známky*),
which can also be bought at
kiosks and some hotels. It may
be possible to send a telegram
from your hotel, too. The
orange and blue letter boxes
are not free-standing but are
hung from the walls of
buildings. *Poste Restante*
communications should be
addressed to Pošta 1 plus the
name of the town.

Public Transport
Communism's emphasis on
community facilities combined
with a relatively low level of

The Church of Sv Jakub in Kutná
Hora, east of Prague

DIRECTORY

private car ownership gave the country a wonderfully comprehensive if somewhat run-down system of public transport. As government subsidies are withdrawn and the need for massive new investment becomes apparent, the future of the system has been thrown into doubt.

Rail

The rail network operated by ČD (České státní dráhy) in Bohemia and Moravia is one of the densest in Europe, and most places of any size have a railway station (*nádraží*), while major cities may have several stations in addition to the main station (*hlavní nádraží*). The hilly nature of the country led to many routes being laid out on a tortuous alignment, so that although you can get virtually anywhere, it may take some time, especially on one of the numerous rural branch lines. Most main lines are electrified, while the branches are operated by diesel railcars and railbuses. 'Rationalisation' of the network is currently under consideration, so services may be cut and lines closed.

A train is either an express (*rychlík*) with first and second class carriages, or a 'people train' ie a slow train (*osobní vlak*), normally with second class only. Fares are rising but are still very low in comparison with Western countries; travelling first class is an option worth considering even if you wouldn't dream of it at home. As well as an ordinary ticket, a trip on most express trains requires a place ticket

(*místenka*). Now that the country has shrunk, you are unlikely to travel anywhere by sleeping car or couchette. Still with some shreds of railway romanticism clinging to it, the overnight express between Prague and the Tatras is now, strictly speaking, an international train. Most stations have detailed information displayed about train times. The easiest to decipher are the white and yellow sheets summarising arrival and departure information respectively.

Bus

The web of bus services is even more densely woven than that of the railway, and there are few settlements that cannot be reached by bus, though not necessarily at a convenient time. Most towns have a bus station (*autobusové nádraží*); the one at Florenc in Prague is particularly impressive. Intermediate stops are identified by a jazzy metal sign marked *zastávka*. The old nationalised company ČSAD still provides the bulk of services, though there is an increasing number of private operators. Fares compare favourably with those on the railway; tickets are bought from kiosks or from the driver. Some cities also have tramway systems and trolleybuses.

Air

Domestic air travel is in the main limited to executive-type flights linking Prague with a small number of major centres such as Brno, Ostrava and Karlovy Vary.

Transport in Prague

Based on metro, tram and bus, the capital's integrated and efficient public transport system shifts two and a half million passengers a day and will get you cheaply to virtually everywhere you need to go, though it is overcrowded at peak times and parts of it are in dire need of investment. Tickets are the same for all three modes. They must be bought in advance from newspaper kiosks, tobacconists and at metro stations and validated by clipping as you enter a station or board a vehicle. A change of mode (*eg* from metro to tram) necessitates validating a new ticket. Single tickets are very inexpensive; consider buying a tourist pass for one to five days if you are going to use public transport frequently.
Metro Long in the planning, Prague's mostly underground Metro had to be redesigned in

Travelling by tram

the aftermath of the 1968 invasion in order to accommodate heavy Soviet-pattern rolling stock in place of the lightweight Italian-type cars that had been foreseen. At present the system consists of three lines: Line A (orange) Dejvická-Skalka, Line B (green) Nové Butovice-Českomoravská and Line C (red) Holešovice-Háje. There are interchange stations in the city centre at Mustek (lower end of Wenceslas Square), Muzeum (top end of Wenceslas Square) and Florenc (main coach station). The metro is clean, swift and safe.
Trams Tram jams used to be common before this venerable means of transport was relieved by the Metro. Tramway routes now fill most of the gaps left by the metro. If you don't want to toil up the steep streets and steps to Hradčany castle, take

one of the trams (no 22) from Malostranská Metro station up tree-lined Mariánské hradby and get off at the castle's rear entrance, the bridge called Prašný most.

Bus Buses mostly function as distributors from the suburban metro stations into the furthest recesses of the high-rise estates that surround the city.

Taxis There is no shortage of taxis in Prague and they are not – or should not be – expensive. You can pick one up from one of the many taxi ranks, hail one on the street (if its sign is illuminated), or phone 02 202 951. Establish an approximate price and ensure that the meter is switched on.

Senior Citizens

There are few concessions for senior citizens apart from free travel on public transport in Prague for the over-70s. As a relatively cheap tourist destination, the Czech Republic could be tempting to anyone on a limited budget.

Student and Youth Travel

The local specialists in all aspects of travel for young people are CKM, at Zitná 12, Praha 2, (tel: 02 299 949), or at Česká 11, Brno (tel: 05 23 641). They can arrange cheap accommodation in youth hostels and hotels and in student residences outside term-time, as well as organising working holidays, stays with families and so on. With an international student identity card you can get concessions on entry to galleries and museums. In Prague, some

foreign youngsters tend to gravitate around the American Hospitality Centre, which is at Malé náměsti 14, Praha 1 (tel: 02 367 486).

Telephones

It's often more convenient to telephone from your hotel, but this will cost more than using a kiosk. Local calls can be made from any kiosk, international calls from those coloured grey. A plentiful supply of coins will be necessary as these calls are not cheap. Phone cards and the phones to take them are beginning to appear. An alternative is to go to a post office and book a call. Give the clerk the full number you want to call and wait until your name is announced. Pay the clerk when the call is completed.

Dialling Codes	
Australia	0061
Eire	00353
New Zealand	0064
UK	0044
US and Canada	001

Time

The Czech Republic regulates its affairs according to Central European Time, one hour ahead of GMT, seven hours ahead of US Standard Time. Clocks are put forward one hour between March and late September.

Tipping

In what is still a low wage country, tips are expected. It is customary to round up the bill at a restaurant or give 10 per cent, likewise when paying a taxi driver. Tour guides and hotel porters should be given a modest consideration, and lavatory attendants a crown or two even if this is not actually demanded.

Toilets

Public toilets are a rarity, indicated by the signs WC, Muži or Páni (men) and Ženy or Dámy (women). Plan your stops around the facilities provided by the places you are likely to be in during the day, your hotel, the café or the restaurant, gallery or museum. Don't forget to tip the guardian of the facilities, from whom you may have to purchase paper.

Tourist Offices

The monolithic state travel agency, Čedok, has been privatised as well as having to split its assets between Czech and Slovak organisations. It is also subject to competition from other travel bureaux

(Autotourist, Alltours, Orea, Rekrea). But with offices all over the country it's still the best place to contact for information as well as tours of many different kinds.

Čedok in the UK 49 Southwark Street, London SE1 1RU (tel: 071 378 6009)
Čedok in the US 10 E 40th Street, New York, NY 10016 (tel: 212 689 9720)
Čedok in Prague Na Příkopě 18, Praha 1 (tel: 02 212 71 11)
Prague Information Office (Pražská informacní služba), Na Příkopě 20, Praha 1 (tel: 02 54 44 44)
CKM, Žitná 12, Praha 2 (tel: 02 29 99 49) specialises in youth travel (see **Student and Youth Travel**)
Balnea, Pařížská 11, Praha 1 (tel: 02 232 19 38) specialises in accommodation and treatment in the spa towns.

Sunset over Prague

LANGUAGE

Czech is one of the family of
Slavonic languages which
includes Russian, though its
closest relatives are Slovak and
Polish. Like all these languages,
it has a complex grammar, and
some of its sounds are not
particularly easy for foreigners
to master. Unless you know
another Slavonic language,
most of the words you
encounter will have an
unfamiliar look, though on
closer inspection similarities
may become apparent,
especially with German. Many
words bristle with accents, and
the spoken language has a very
distinct sound because of the
prevalence of consonants.
Czechs enjoy making up
tongue-twisting sentences
without using a single vowel!
As in any country, it's
worthwhile mastering a few
phrases of the language, even if
only to be able to enquire
politely if anyone understands
your own; making yourself
familiar with some commonly
encountered signs will help in
finding your way round.

Pronounciation

Whatever difficulties Czech
may present, it has the
advantage of being
pronounced as it is written. The
stress is always on the first
syllable of the word.

Vowels

á	as in father
é	as in air
ě	as in yes
í, ý	as in meet
o	as in more
ů	as in boom

Consonants

c	as in its
č	as in china
ch	as in loch
j	as in yes
ň	as in onion
r	Scottish r
ř	unique to Czech, a combination of r and z (try Dvořák)
š	as in shine
z	as in zero
ž	as in pleasure

Useful words

chrám large church or
  cathedral
col customs
cukrárna patisserie
divadlo theatre
dům house
hranice border
hora mountain
hospoda/hostinec pub
hrad castle (fortified)
informace information
kaple chapel
kavárna café
klášter monastery
kostel church
lahůdky delicatessen
lekárna pharmacy
malý/á/é small
město town
most bridge
nádraži station
hlavní nádraži main station
autobusové nádraži bus
  station
náměstí square
nový/á/é new
pivnice pub
pivo beer
potraviny supermarket
pozor! danger!
restaurace restaurant
sem pull (sign on door)

směnárna *bureau de change*
starý/á/é old
tam push (sign on door)
trh market
třída avenue
ulice street
věž tower
vinárna wine bar
velký/á/é big
voda water
víno wine
vchod/vstup entrance
východ/výstup exit
zahrada garden
zakázáno forbidden
zámek castle/country house
zastávka bus stop

Basic Words and Phrases

yes ano
no ne
please prosím
thank you děkuji
do you speak
   English/German?
   mluvíte anglicky/německy?
I don't understand nerozumím
I don't speak Czech nemluvím
   česky
hello ahoj
good morning dobrý den
good evening dobrý večer
good night dobrou noc
goodbye na shledanou
sorry promiňte
where? kde?
how much? kolik?
when? když?
what? co?

Numbers

1	jeden/jedna/jedno
2	dva/dvě
3	tři
4	čtyři
5	pět
6	šest
7	sedm
8	osm
9	devět
10	deset
11	jedenáct
12	dvanáct
13	třináct
14	čtyřnáct
15	patnáct
16	šestnáct
17	sedmnáct
18	osmnáct
19	devatenáct
20	dvacet
30	třicet
40	čtyřicet
50	padesát
60	šedesát
70	sedmdesát
80	osmdesát
90	devadesát
100	sto
1,000	tisíc

Days of the Week

Monday pondělí
Tuesday úterý
Wednesday středa
Thursday čvrtek
Friday pátek
Saturday sobota
Sunday neděle

Months of the Year

Czech uses poetic names for its months, *eg* January is *leden* (the icy one), November is *listopad* (leaf-fall).

January leden
February únor
March březen
April duben
May květen
June červen
July červenec
August srpen
September září
October říjen
November listopad
December prosinec

INDEX

INDEX/ACKNOWLEDGEMENTS

Acknowledgements

The Automobile Association wishes to thank the following photographer
and libraries for their assistance in the preparation
of this book.

Jon Wyand took all the photographs (© AA Photo Library) except for:

MARY EVANS PICTURE LIBRARY *7* view of Prague

THE NATURE PHOTOGRAPHERS LTD *91* Military orchid (R. Bush), *92* Great
spotted woodpecker (P. R. Sterry), *94* Edible frog (P. R. Sterry), *95* Eagle owl
(E. A. Janes)

SPECTRUM COLOUR LIBRARY *89* Piešťany, *96* Strbské Pleso

Series adviser: Christopher Catling   Copy editor: Nia Williams
Verifiers: Jenny Fry & Dr Christopher Rice   Indexer: Marie Lorimer